This book

- You think there may be a book inside you but you are not sure

- You have been speaking in public for years and people keep asking you for your book - and you haven't got round to writing it yet

- You have a website full of articles and blogs and they are not making you a penny!

- You need a book to help launch your career as a platform presenter

- Everybody knows that you are an expert on your specialist subject and you spend your time giving advice on it to others. Then somebody said, "You ought to write a book."

- You have spent a lifetime training others and have amassed invaluable knowledge and experience that you want to pass on

- You have climbed the ladder of success and want to help others to do the same.

If you have spent a lifetime making deposits into your Bank of Knowledge, there isn't a better time than now to make a withdrawal, and convert it into a form that others can recognise its value to them and to buy it.

Let me help you to turn your Knowledge into Income.

About the author

Chris Day's career in communications started in live theatre as an actor as well as in stage management and technical production. With seasons in the West End, with the National Theatre and also in the Provinces, he has also appeared in films, on radio and on television.

In Scotland he was responsible for promotions and publicity for a number of theatres and venues and later become the first Tourism and Conference Promotions Officer in the PR department of the City of Glasgow.

In between everything he has also grown a successful chain of retail shops, which he later sold, and which is still operating today.

In the late 1980s, looking for a new challenge he joined Encyclopaedia Britannica in sales. He progressed into sales management as a national trainer and finally running the Field Training and Communications department. When the company restructured, he founded his own media production company, which then grew into his current business, Filament Publishing, Media and Marketing.

Today, as a publisher, he helps people realise the value of their knowledge and experience, and works with them to turn it into books and knowledge based products, and then to successfully market them to their niche.

Chris writes a monthly column for Making Money Magazine and also holds workshops and training events for new authors.

For more information go to www.AskChrisDay.com and
www.filamentpublishing.com

Turning your Knowledge into Income

Practical advice on how to create and market knowledge based products

by Chris Day

With expert contributions from

Brian Mayne, Ron G Holland
David Barber, John S Rushton
Colin Bennett, Phil Chambers
David White, Ray Hodges
Rachael Ross, Frazer Ashford
Zara Thatcher and Jonathan Jay

Published by
Filament Publishing Ltd
14, Croydon Road,
Waddon, Croydon
Surrey CR0 4PA
Telephone +44(0)20 8688 2598
info@filamentpublishing.com
www.filamentpublishing.com

ISBN 978-1-905493-40-1

Printed by Advanced Document Solutions, Uxbridge
Distributed by Gardners

A free online course which includes material from this book
can be found on www.authors-course.com

I would like to dedicate this book

To my wife Rosemary

To Jonathan Jay, one of the most
original, talented and dynamic
entrepreneurs I have ever met

and

To Joe D Adams for his generosity in
sharing opportunity and of inspiring
countless people to discover things
in themselves they doubted were there.

To each of you,
Thank you

Acknowledgements

I would like to thank all of my expert contributors who were good enough to share their knowledge and insights.

Brian Mayne, the originator of Goal Mapping. You can try it free of charge at www.liftinternational.com

Ron G Holland, author of *The Eureka! Enigma*
See www.wealth.co.uk

David Barber, author of the popular *Living with Heart* series
www.davidbarberbooks.com

John S Rushton, broadcaster and author of *Love Your Life*, part of the *Alchemy of Life* series. www.thelifealchemist.com

Phil Chambers, the Mind Mapping World Champion
www.learning-tech.co.uk

David White, the CEO of Weboptimiser
www.weboptimiser.com

Ray Hodges, Senior PR Consultant, HPS Media Group
www.hpsgroup.co.uk

Rachael Ross, author of *How to Make Working From Home Work For You* www.purelypeppermint.com

Colin Bennett, author and playwright www.acquiredtastetv.co.uk

Frazer Ashford ABIPP ARPS www.frazerashford.com

Zara Thatcher www.filamentpublishing.com

Jonathan Jay, SuccessTrack www.successtrackonline.com
and National Association of Business Owners www.nabo.biz

"The only way to get what you want,

is to help enough other people

to get what they want"

Zig Ziglar

Table of Contents

TURNING YOUR KNOWLEDGE INTO INCOME............................ 11

PART ONE - KNOW WHAT YOU KNOW............................. 19

Do you know what you know?...................................... 21

"I'm not sure I want to make money from my book...".................. 24

So, who are you?.. 27

"So is there a market for what I know?"........................... 30

Questions are the key.. 32

The Big Question to ask yourself................................. 33

So what's the plan?... 35

"Will I be able to write a book?" By David Barber...................... 38

Learning from the School of Life by Brian Mayne...................... 48

The secret to making money from your books and information products by Jonathan Jay................................... 56

PART TWO - GROW WHAT YOU KNOW........................... 67

Real cash in the attic.. 70

Scary movies... 70

Mind Mapping for Authors by Phil Chambers......................... 72

Working From Home Guide For Authors by Rachael Ross............. 78

Your New Best Friend.. 84

Your Support Team.. 87

How do we overcome the Magnets of Immediate Desires?......... 91

Writing not Wronging! By Colin Bennett............................. 93

The Write Stuff by David Barber................................... 100

Through the eyes of a Proofreader by Zara Thatcher................. 106

My Journey into Publishing as an Author by John S Rushton....... 112

Laying out your book on the page................................. 117

Never Judge a Book by its Cover - Wrong! By Frazer Ashford...... 133

PART THREE - SHARE WHAT YOU KNOW......................... 141

Is Social Media relevant to business? By David White............... 143

Marketing your book - and then some! By Ron G Holland........... 154

Mounting a PR Campaign by Ray Hodges........................... 158

Radio interviews.. 167
How massive book sales are really created! By Ron G Holland... 168
Marketing the book.. 171
The Newsletter Trap.. 173
Getting tangled in the web... 176
Adding Value... 176
When is a book not a book?... 178
Joint Ventures... 180
And finally... 183

"Success is nothing more than a few simple disciplines, practiced every day, whilst failure is simply a few errors of judgement, repeated every day.

It is the accumulative weight of our disciples and our judgements that leads us to either fortune or failure"

Jim Rohn

Turning your Knowledge into Income

**Share what you know - help others grow,
and Turn your Knowledge into Income**

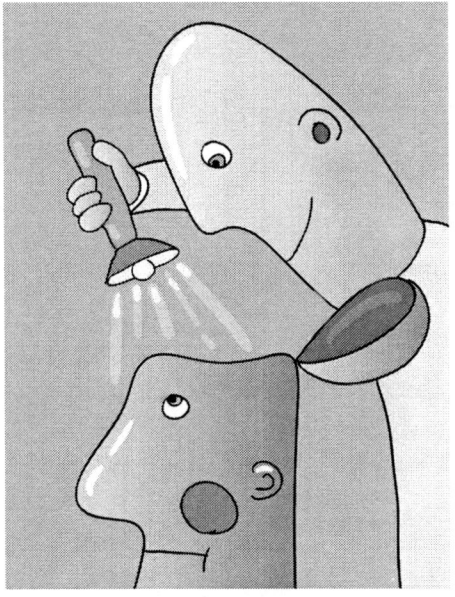

I'd like to invite you on a journey of discovery. Actually it's a bit of a treasure hunt. I believe that hidden inside every brain is a dusty area covered in cobwebs containing long forgotten knowledge, past experiences, skills and old qualifications that haven't seen the light of day for quite some time.

All knowledge has a value and sometimes all it takes is a question for it all to flood right back to the surface, ready to be of use again.

It is this valuable knowledge that has the potential of earning you some income. I might be wrong. It might be the case that if I were to wade through your deepest thoughts, I wouldn't get my feet wet. But on the other hand I might be right - and if I am, you'll kick yourself for not doing something about it.

Most people spend a lifetime making regular deposits into their personal Bank of Knowledge and build up considerable assets.

Very often when they are looking to cash in on other physical assets and dig themselves out of a hole, they completely overlook the most valuable things they own - their knowledge, experience and the insights that they have had over the years. By forgetting about them you are, in effect, letting your Bank of Knowledge have a dormant account!

Now, you could be a specialist trainer or consultant in any one of countless industries and make your living by sharing your knowledge with others.

You may already be an acknowledged expert in your field and drowning under a wealth of articles, speeches, recordings, and videos of your performances, and are looking for help to turn this valuable resource into books and products.

Alternatively, you may just have a small spark of an idea and need help to coax it out into the light, give it some kindling, and to turn it into a flame. But right now you don't know where to start and need help with the basics.

In the following chapters, I have tried to accommodate the needs of both the professional communicator as well as the first time author. So, when you start a section, and discover it is a flash of the blindingly obvious, you do have my permission to skip to the next section, which will hopefully be more relevant to your needs. You will not need to bring a note from a responsible adult and I won't be upset.

So if you are ready, and if you have remembered to bring a packed lunch and a clean handkerchief, let's set out on our journey into the deepest vaults of your brain. We'll be going past the bit that is still running repeats of *The Likely Lads* and *Rising Damp* with Leonard Rossiter, and round the corner from all those embarrassing outtakes of your life that you'd rather forget. Please don't get distracted.

I know you doubt very much that there is anything of value down there, but you might be surprised. After all, they did manage to find enough material for sixteen series of *Cash in the Attic*!

Before I forget, this book is in three parts, but I reserve the right to tack on a few extra bits on the way. If, when we are halfway through, I have tantalised you with a thought or idea, but not developed it enough for you, I'd invite you to go to www.authors-course.com where I have added all the bits I had meant to put into the book but thought of them too late.

Alternatively, I am more than happy to receive an email to chris@askchrisday.com I might even surprise you with an answer! I have also invited a number of experts and successful published authors, who I really respect, to share their knowledge and experience. You will find their articles scattered throughout the book.

As they say, if you want to know what lies ahead on the road, ask someone who is walking towards you.

You will hear from international author, and the originator of Goal Mapping, Brian Mayne about the hurdles he had to overcome before he could start writing. Anthony Robbins said of him, "Brian is one of the best at helping people create a world-class blueprint for their life, not just goals but sustainable success. His Mapping Systems are a blast and really effective."

Author David Barber has written or ghost-written 30 books and many business manuals, has been translated into almost 20 languages and has written the popular *Living with Heart* series of books. He writes about the question uppermost on most people's minds: "Will I be able to write a book?"

Colin Bennett, the actor, author and playwright, provides an insight into the process of writing in his own quirky style. A RADA trained actor, he is most famous for his role as Mr Bennett, the accident prone caretaker and straightman for Tony Hart in the BBC children's programmes *Take Hart* and *Hartbeat*. He also portrayed the father in the 1985 Yellow Pages/Hornby advert *Signal Box*.

Professional photographer Frazer Ashford asks the question "Do you judge a book by its cover?" and provides some useful information about the art of taking photographs for a book.

Zara Thatcher, a member of the Society for Editors and Proofreaders and a member of the in-house editorial team at Filament Publishing, gives practical advice on making sure that your book is accurate and free of errers.(!)

PR is an area which many profess expertise, but few deliver. We are very fortunate to have an article from Ray Hodges. Ray has 30 years of experience in PR, and ran two successful and nationally recognised PR agencies. She now operates her own PR boutique out of the HPS Group, one of the biggest marketing communications agencies in the south of England.

Phil Chambers is the Mind Mapping World Champion. Who better to explain this invaluable tool for authors to help organise their content. Invented by Tony Buzan, Mind Mapping is now available as a powerful online tool from www.thinkBuzan.com and is highly recommended by many authors.

Rachael Ross is the author of *How to Make Working From Home Work For You*. She contributes an article of practical ideas to help an author to get organised in their home office. You'll discover that common sense is far from common. It is the obvious that eludes us all.

Book Marketing is also an art in itself and there is no one better at it than international author Ron G Holland who is acclaimed as Britain's Leading Motivational Speaker, Top Biz Guru and the Entrepreneur's Entrepreneur with an international reputation. He is the author of many business books and manuals, including *Talk & Grow Rich, Turbo Success* and The *Eureka! Enigma*.

His highly acclaimed audio programmes include *Escape From Where I Am* and are in every prison library in the UK.

A growing tool that authors are increasingly relying on is Social Networking. I am therefore delighted that David White, the CEO of Weboptimiser Ltd and an international expert on Social Networking for business, has also contributed an invaluable article.

I am indebted to writer and broadcaster John Rushton, who wrote the *Alchemy of Life* series. His book *Love Your Life* is helping countless people finding themselves at Life's Crossroads. He shares his experience as an author in his very helpful article.

Jonathan Jay is a multi-millionaire entrepreneur and marketing maverick obsessed with helping business owners to reach their potential. He's the Chairman of the National Association of Business Owner, the founder and Managing Director of SuccessTrack and the founder of The Coaching Academy UK. He is the author of three books (including *Sack Your Boss*), the star of  TV's *Now I'm The Boss*, a magazine publisher (*The Achievement Report* and award-winning *Personal Success*), and a popular and in-demand speaker, as well as being the UK's highest-paid business consultant.

I am very grateful to all these talented and generous people for sharing their wisdom. I have learnt a lot from them. I have included links to their various websites on the acknowledgement page.

Finally, many people buy books and don't read them. They believe that, just by owning them, the knowledge will mysteriously transfer to them whilst it sits on the shelf. I think of it as 'Shelf Development'.

So, rather than make an ornament out of it, or use it to make your desk level, I'd like to encourage you to use this as a workbook. Do make notes in the margin. Do use a highlighter pen. Do turn down the corners on the book. It is there to be used.

In fact, the more you abuse the book, the more likely it will fall apart and you'll have to buy another one. You see, it's purely selfish!

Oh yes! In case you'd thought I'd forgotten, the three parts of the book are:

Part One	Know what you know - discover what is hidden inside your vault of knowledge.
Part Two	Grow what you know - discover the practical steps you need to take to extract what you know and repurpose it into a form that you can share with others at a profit to yourself.
Part Three	Share what you know - how to identify your niche and to market yourself and your products.

So, if you are up for it, grab your Wellingtons and a torch - we are about to dive in. It could be a bit messy in there, and we might be some time.....

**Napoleon didn't get to Moscow by
putting on a blindfold,
sticking a pin in the map
and then getting on his horse.
He had a plan.**

**Unfortunately for him, he had
no plan for getting back**

EXPERTS IN THEIR FIELD.

Part One - Know what you know

Knowledge on its own is not enough to make you rich. If it were, then every academic would be driving a Porsche, not a bicycle. Having knowledge and successfully turning that into its full income potential are two different things.

If you have spent a lifetime working in any profession or industry, you will have built up knowledge and experience that would be invaluable to anybody joining that industry today. And they would willingly pay to learn the shortcuts and avoid the pitfalls that await them. To them, you are the expert.

So what is an expert? An expert is someone who is perceived to know more about a particular subject than others. The keyword here is 'perceived'. In reality, they may not be the most knowledgeable or the best qualified, but they have achieved sufficient profile to have become recognised as a reliable source of specialist information and informed opinion on their chosen subject.

But achieving expert status doesn't happen just because you have the knowledge and experience, in the same way that having the best mousetrap in the world and doing nothing with it. Knowledge won't make you any money unless you package it into a form that can be marketed and sold. There are many other ways of marketing your knowledge than just writing a book, as you will discover.

What difference could it make to you in your business right now if you were a published author with a book that identified you as an expert in your field?

- Would your customers think about you in a different way?
- How would your competitors think about you?
- How would your industry now view you?
- How would the media view you?
- How would you view yourself?
- What would you be doing differently?

Being a published author makes a disproportionate difference. It shouldn't do, but it does. In these competitive times, it can really give you the edge!

Do you know what you know?

It might seem an odd question because, on the face of it, of course we know what we know! But do we really? I often joke that I've forgotten more than I knew in the first place, but then somebody asks a question, and you trawl back in your brain to something you knew a long time ago, and surprise, surprise, that little piece of knowledge was there all along. We all know far more than we believe we do, sometimes all we need are the questions to help tease it out.

Your 'neck top' computer is the most amazing thing on earth because it can create the most powerful thing on earth - a thought! Don't believe me? Just take a look at history.

It takes just one thought, giving space enough to grow into a fully fledged idea, then properly nurtured, presented and shared with other people, and hitherto unimagined things can be caused to happen.

Every major building or engineering project started as - just one tiny thought.

Every great advance in science started as - just one tiny thought.

Every action, good or bad, is in response to - just one tiny thought.

Thinking is the most powerful thing we can ever do.

Sow a thought - and reap a thoughtune!

One little thought in the mind of printer Colin Macfarquhar in Edinburgh in 1768 grew into an idea for a comprehensive dictionary of all known knowledge. He shared the idea with his friend, Andrew Bell, an engraver, and together they hired a Fellow of the Royal Society, William Smellie, to write it for them, which he did, in 100 weekly instalments. Not a lot of people know that!

Almost two hundred and fifty years later, the Encyclopaedia Britannica is now the world's most respected source of knowledge, available in almost every language and now available online twenty four hours a day. But it started as just one little thought, shared with others, and turned into a plan of action. If one man can write the three original volumes of Encyclopaedia Britannica in two years without the help of a computer, what could you achieve these days in a fraction of the time? Maybe now is a good time to dig out your book of plausible excuses?

Many good ideas started out as a little frustration. Someone was having difficulty trying to perform a particular task, or was looking for a piece of information and said, "Now if only there was a book about this!" - and out of that need, an idea was born.

In reality, most people underrate their knowledge and certainly don't believe it has any value to anyone else. It is also a fact that, for some people, at the time when they need to call on it the most and turn it into income, they are probably at a point in their life when they have been made redundant or are at a career crossroads and are at their least confident. Having suffered a loss of confidence, very often a lack of self belief and self worth also follows. So if life hasn't treated you well recently and you feel that way, then first remind yourself of how good you actually are.

When your last employer saw you for the first time, they knew right away that you could add value to their business. You had then - and have now - skills, talents, experience, knowledge, qualities and qualifications that they recognised as valuable, and which are still just as valuable now. You brought a lot to their table and they paid you the minimum they could get away with in order to persuade you to work for them. They went on to make a profit from your contribution to their success. You are valuable. You are good. They were lucky to have you and it is very much their loss that you are no longer there.

You are still the same person that you were when you went to that first interview. You still have those same skills, talents and qualities. But now, you have considerably more experience, and a track record that you didn't have before. You are now even more valuable - not less! Your task now is to find a way of converting those not inconsiderable assets into income. Now is the time for action, not to have a pity party.

How many times have you heard someone say, "If I had a pound for every good idea I've had, I would be a rich man!" and obviously they are not! A lesson there possibly? Having powerful thoughts and good ideas happens to everybody but it is only those very few who are prepared who act on them, and who will reap the rewards of doing so. Action is the key!

Are you just a thinker or a talker? Or do you put thoughts into action? Your knowledge, information, experience, and personal insights that could be very helpful to somebody who is now treading the same path that you once trod. You have the choice of letting all of that knowledge fritter away, or you could choose to capture it and harvest its potential. So here is an important piece of advice.

Use it or lose it!

"I'm not sure I want to make money from my book..."

Of course, not everybody wants to write for money, in fact for most authors the money is secondary. Their motivation is simply to share their knowledge and help other people. This is all very well, but nobody can live on fresh air. I am all for being philanthropic, but you can only be so if you are able to care for your own basic needs first.

One person I have the highest regard for is author Brian Mayne, who originated the concept of Goal Mapping. He has had more than his fair share of difficulties and challenges in his life and he also has a great attitude of abundance.

He is never slow to offer training and seminars to schools and those in need at no charge. However, he rightly commands appropriate fees when training in companies and for his platform presenting, which subsides all the good work he does elsewhere.

A great example of how to get the balance right. Incidentally his newly released online Goal Mapping tool can be found on www.liftinternational.com and it's free to use! It will also be a big help for you in prioritising your goals, should you choose to take your project further.

If you are still struggling with the idea of being commercial and of writing for money, remember what the famous American trainer and motivator Zig Ziglar famously said.

"You can have anything you want in life if you help enough other people to get what they want."

What a powerful concept.

So, if you are to embark on a journey to turn your thoughts into a book, what new doors could that also open for you? You could use the fact that you have become a published author to launch a new career as a public speaker, or to be seen as an expert in your field.

Getting a book published is just a stepping stone to help you achieve what it is you really want in life. Very often publishing a book will unlock other income opportunities that would not have been possible without it.

Whatever your big goal is, my focus will be to help you to achieve it in as low cost a way as possible, and to help you to find ways of generating new income streams as quickly as possible.

You'll be surprised at how many ways you can repurpose what you know into a whole portfolio of products, and there are countless examples of people to inspire you who have done just that.

If you are not quite sure where to start, whether you are capable of writing, or indeed whether anybody would ever be interested in reading it, let's start at the very beginning. Let's spend 30 seconds on your specialist subject - you!

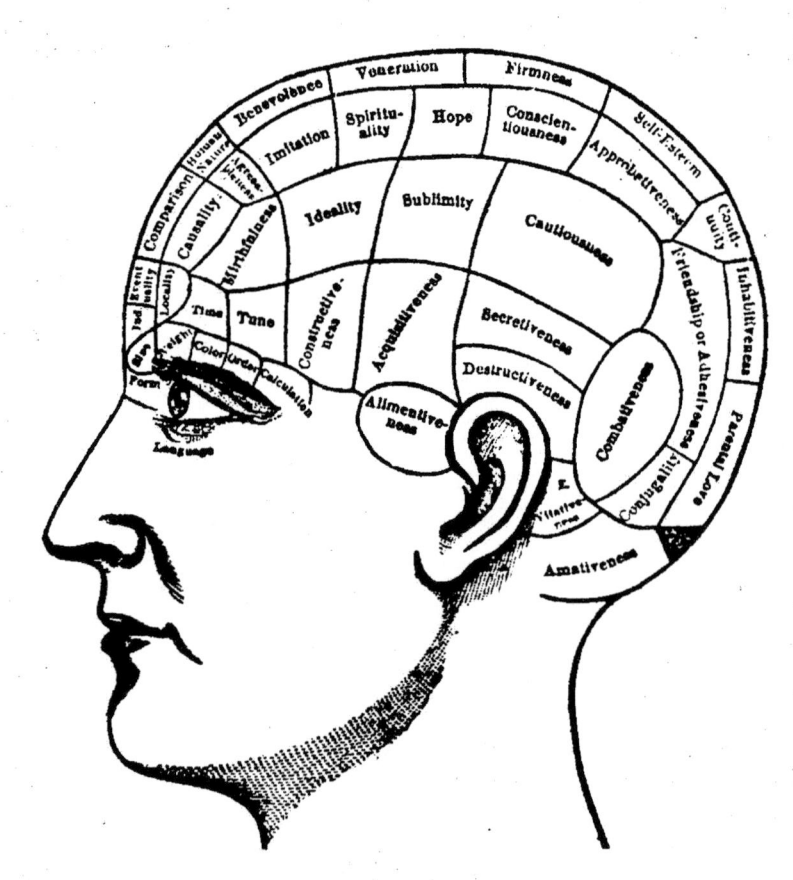

So, who are you?

In an era where the concept of a job for life seems to be a quaint piece of history, the chances are that you have been many different people over your life. People refer to their CV as a 'portfolio' of all the experience and the different skills they have mastered as they reinvent themselves, moving from job to job or from opportunity to opportunity. It is very easy to forget everything you have done and all the latent knowledge hidden inside you.

Step one, therefore, in your journey of inner discovery is to create a timeline of all the different people you have been. This should not be confined to just the jobs you have done, but should also include the different hobbies or interests you have had and the different roles you have fulfilled. For example, you may have been a carer for a sick relative, or you may have adopted children. Both roles would have given you an insight into the challenges that might be faced by others doing the same thing in the future. What did you discover that might help them?

Our interests change over the years and a hobby that might have fascinated us years ago may well now be almost forgotten. When I was a youngster, in the middle ages, I lived in a seaside resort that attracted coach loads of visitors from all over the UK.

My hobby was to collect bus tickets by asking the visiting drivers if they had any. Sad but true. For years I kept albums of them in the loft. Recently I typed the phrase 'Collecting transport tickets' into Google and, much to my amazement, discovered there was a website for The Transport Ticket Society. I found out it was founded in 1946, has 380 members worldwide and a magazine of their own. All of a sudden, I discovered I am an expert in an area I had forgotten all about.

Now I do have to admit that I would find it difficult to make a career out of this highly niche subject, but that is not the point. Had I not gone through this exercise myself, I would never have thought about it. It is only by creating your own timeline, going back as far as you can, that you will unlock memories such as that.

So to start, get yourself a hardback, lined notebook. The bigger, the better. Use it to pin down on paper your memories, your achievements, and your ideas. Putting them on paper is essential. You can't carry it all in your head.

"The faintest of ink is better than the strongest of memory"

At this stage, don't evaluate anything; just record all your thoughts on paper. Put down the important milestone dates and then work around them. As you do so, two or more seemingly random items will suddenly link together into something new. Keep the big picture of what you are looking for in mind, and be alert for new ideas. They are there waiting for you! Here is a list of places to look.

Memory Joggers:

- Old diaries
- Photo albums
- Newspaper cuttings
- Jobs and employers
- Projects you have worked on
- Processes you became expert at
- Achievements you were recognised for
- Awards you received
- Bills
- Letters and emails
- Boxes in the loft or the cellar

- Old address books - who did you know then and why?
- Wage slips
- Courses you have taken
- Qualifications you gained
- Places you have visited in the course of your work or on holiday
- People you have known or worked with - are they famous now?
- Major events that you witnessed or were part of
- Do you have a famous relative?
- What clubs or societies have you belonged to?
- Have your friends kept any records or items?

Memories of particular events can be fascinating for people who were there themselves, or who have a particular interest in them. These can be brought to life if you have any photos, press cuttings or documents which relate to your story or experience.

Look for anything that can unlock a memory. It would be highly unusual if, having gone through this process, you could not find a number of subjects that, with a bit more research and reading up on the subject if necessary, you could become expert in once again.

They say that the only difference between you as an amateur in any subject and you as an expert is time and dedication. If you were to read a book a week on just one subject, after one year you will know far more on that subject than almost anyone else! If you decide to, you can become an expert in almost anything if you are prepared to focus on it and give it time. You will have a head start if you worked in this field in the past, but it is not essential.

But in your quest to unlock the subject which is going to be the one you will be pouring your energy into, there is one quality which, if lacking, will doom your enterprise to failure.

To reinvent yourself as an expert, to write a book, to give talks on the subject, to be interviews by the media, none of these will happen IF you don't have enthusiasm.

> *"When you are on fire with enthusiasm, people will travel for miles to watch you burn!"*

You may not know anything about 17th century porcelain. You may care about it even less but when antiques expert Henry Sandon on the BBC *Antiques Roadshow* was shown 'Ozzy the Owl', which turned out to be a rare piece of Slipware pottery, his enthusiasm for the find and his valuation of £20,000 made captivating viewing.

Your enthusiasm for your specialist subject is what will make you stand out. It is what will make your words worth reading. It is what will make your talks worth listening to. It is what will make your magazine article worth reading.

So what gets you enthusiastic? If you can answer that question, then you have found a firm foundation on which to reinvent yourself. The rest will be easy.

"So is there a market for what I know?"

It use to be the case that, in order to become qualified in a particular profession, you would first become an apprentice, and learn your trade by working with a qualified expert. The process would take a few years and, at the end of it, you would have a rounded knowledge of the subject and be able to turn your hand to virtually any related problem you might face.

These days, to be an expert means learning more and more about less and less.

The days of the all-rounder are gone. What used to be well within the capabilities of one person is now split into a number of smaller areas of expertise, or even professions in their own right. We live in a world of increasingly smaller niches - which is good news! It means that you don't need to know everything about everything; you only need to know everything about something. And that something can be quite small.

So the first step in discovering whether there is a market for your knowledge is to research your niche.

With every idea you have for a book, here are some questions you will need to answer in order to discover if there is a market for it.

- Who would want to know this piece of information?
- Why would they need to know it?
- What would they be trying to accomplish?
- Is this for work or pleasure?
- Where would they go to find this out?
- Who would they ask?
- What books are already out there in this topic?
- Is there an aspect of the subject that is not well covered?
- Do I have something unique to add?
- Who are known experts on this subject?
- What can you learn from them?
- How do they market their knowledge?
- What do people wanting to know this have in common?
- Would they belong to any particular organisation or club?
- Do they have a particular qualification?
- Are they in one geographic area?
- Are they likely to be Internet users?
- What keywords or phrases would they use to search? Do a search yourself to find out!

- What websites cover this topic? Make a list of them and identify the elements on each one that work best.
- What publications do they read?
- Are there exhibitions or events devoted to this topic?

The more you put yourself in the mindset of your potential reader, the more research you do and the more questions you ask people, the easier you will find it to focus on the subject that will generate the most interest and give you the biggest return.

Questions are the key

Earlier on I suggested that questions are a great way of unlocking your knowledge. They are also a great way of tuning in to what people need to know right now. If you are already giving talks on your specialist subject, or have a website devoted to it, look for ways of encouraging people to ask questions. Then, and most importantly, make sure you record or capture both the question and your answer.

If you are giving a talk or seminar, even if you have given that same talk many times in the past, the most valuable thing will be the questions people ask at the end. That is why it is so important to record everything you say in public - or you will lose the opportunity to transcribe those valuable words.

Speaking of which, many acknowledged experts throw away so much priceless information by not capturing it. Every time you are speaking to a live audience, there is a very special dynamic that doesn't happen anywhere else. The adrenaline of the moment, the focus you have on your subject, the pressure of performing in front of a live audience; they all work together to bring out the best in us all. If you don't record, you are depriving yourself of revisiting and reusing those golden words in the future, especially all the questions you will be asked! Record everything and build up an archive of material you will be able to draw from in the future.

The Big Question to ask yourself

In 1902, author Rudyard Kipling wrote a series of cautionary tales called the *Just So Stories*. In one of these, titled *How the Elephant got its trunk*, was a little piece of wisdom that has been the mantra for professional journalists ever since.

"I keep six honest serving-men: (They taught me all I knew) Their names are What and Where and When, And How and Why and Who."

Whether you are writing a news article or planning a project, you need to satisfy the needs of each of these six simple words and the most important one right now is "Why?"

The bigger your "why?", the easier it will be to successfully complete the project. Conversely, if you don't have a really good reason to do this, you will get bored with it very quickly and quietly forget about it. So what is your reason?

Of course, there are many people who will have never asked themselves that question but still go on to spend hours upon hours slaving over a keyboard and successfully overcome all the obstacles to create their book.

Having then gone through all the process of getting a cover designed, the book typeset and finally published, they then lost interest and did nothing with it. What a waste of all that effort! An entire industry has grown up called 'Vanity Publishing' to help people with more money than sense to do just that.

Why are you planning to put yourself through all of this effort and heartache? Writing a book is a real rollercoaster ride of ups and downs. There will be many times when you'll find it too difficult and want to give up. Your brain will go on strike and all of those many jobs around the house that you have been putting off will suddenly look really appealing. It is only if the reason that you are doing this is large enough that you will find the motivation to keep going.

Everybody's reason will be different. You may have been made redundant and you want to reinvent yourself as a consultant. Being a published author will certainly give you credibility in your marketplace.

It may be that you are already a huge success in your own right and busier than you could believe. Creating a range of books and products based on your knowledge can really leverage your time and create a residual income that could enable you to be a bit more selective as to how you use your time. It could also mean that you can put your prices up and work less hard.

Whatever your reason, write it down on the first page of your notebook. Whenever you are tempted to walk away, turn back to that page and remind yourself of it. The bigger the reason, the more powerful will be the motivation to get it finished, and for you to move closer to achieving that goal. Don't forget to use the free Goal Mapping software from Brian Mayne that I mentioned earlier as well. It will also make a big difference.

The question you need to answer then is "What will being a published author help me to achieve?" Only when you can truthfully answer that is it worth reading on and taking the next step.

For example, becoming a published author might;

1. Give me additional profile in my marketplace
2. Give a competitive edge to my business
3. Allow me to help others to achieve what I have done
4. Create opportunities for public speaking engagements
5. Help me to be perceived as an expert
6. Generate a residual income
7. Help others to cope with a particular set of circumstances
8. Make it easier to sell my other services or products
9. Attract interest from the media
10. Help me to leave a worthwhile legacy of knowledge

So what is important to you? You need to know because with every project you need to start with the end in mind!

So what's the plan?

As the legendary motivational speaker, coach and author Brian Tracy says most people live in a place called 'Someday Isle'. You ask them what their plans for the future are and they'll tell you, "Someday I'll write a book" or "Someday I'll make the time to follow my dreams." But, for the majority, Someday Isle is a place they will never actually visit, because they never make a plan to get there.

Of course, they all have well rehearsed reasons for not going there, but in reality they are just excuses, and their dreams remain as distant as ever.

The fact that you are reading this suggests that you may have run out of these excuses, and find yourself ready to take action to start to move towards achieving your long held dreams. If that is the case, congratulations! The good news is that by making the decision to "just do it!", you may well find that what you thought was going to be a massive mountain to climb may only be a foothill. Nothing is actually as difficult as we think it is going to be before we get started.

Of course, it may also be that your dreams are still a bit vague, and you need a bit of help to clearly visualise them. And that is fine as well. No matter what it is you really want to do, the clearer and more specific it is, the easier it will be to achieve.

For example, if your goal is "to earn some more money", how will you know when you have earned enough? On the other hand, if your goal is to earn an extra £100 per week, then you have something very specific to do - and you will have the satisfaction of knowing that you have achieved your goal when you get there. Having the discipline to achieve a small goal then gives you the confidence to achieve a larger one. Writing a book for example might appear to be a daunting task, but it starts by writing just one sentence. And then another one. And then another.

No matter how distant your destination, you get there by walking one step at a time - providing you are walking in the right direction! But just having a clear goal, and a plan to achieve it, doesn't mean that you have the motivation to get out of bed and do it. You need a reason. For example, you may be looking to the future and realising that your pension is not going to keep you in the lifestyle to which you have become accustomed.

You might currently have too much month at the end of the money and urgently need to do something about it. Or you might have discovered that your "flexible friends" have suddenly become rather inflexible, and you need to get rid of the card balances that have crept up on you.

If you are to be successful in achieving your goals, you need a big reason. If you know what it is, and it is big enough to drive you, then write it down on a small card and put it in your wallet or purse. Whenever you are faced with the choice of doing what you need to do, or of skiving off instead, take it out and remind yourself of it. If the reason is big enough, it will be sufficient to get you back on track. So the challenge, before going further, is to write down;

- What it is you want to do
- What achieving that will help you to achieve
- The big reason you have for doing it

Once you can answer those questions, you are ready to move forward. But be aware that the key is to write the answers down. Anything that is not written down is just a wish - and wishes are not enough to get you to 'Someday Isle'.

The trouble for each one of us is that "Life gets in the way." If we are planning to do something new, which is going to take time and focus, we need to decide how we are going to integrate that into our current lifestyle. I have discovered to my cost that unless I "plan" to do something, I am actually planning not to do it. If one of your goals involves writing, for example, an important factor is knowing what time of day you are in the most productive frame of mind to do that - and when you are likely to get the least interruptions. For me, I have discovered that getting up early and writing from 6am until 9am works for me. I know other authors who prefer to write late into the evening. We are all different. You need to know your Golden Time.

One person who has overcome all of these obstacles is international author David Barber. David is one of the most insightful writers I know and his books have helped countless people. He answers the one question that you need to know the answer to right now.

"Will I be able to write a book?"
By David Barber

The first question to ask is: if you knew that no one would read your book, would you still want to write it? If the answer is yes, then you are a genuine writer.

The fact is that the majority of titles published by even the mainstream publishers fail (that is why you see so many, even those written by famous writers or well-known personalities, being sold at very big discounts). No matter how saleable you think your book will be, and don't take any notice of what other people or your digital or eBook publisher will say, the probability is that, as a self-publisher and without the expertise and backing of a traditional publishing house, your book is far more likely to fail and will probably sell far fewer copies if it does succeed. There are famous exceptions, of course, but don't rely on yourself being one of them.

People fall into four categories:

1. "I don't think I could write a book!"
2. People who think that just because they are experts in their field or chosen subject, they must per se be able to write about it.
3. People who assume that their English education (meaning a knowledge of grammar and syntax or, even worse, they verbally can string two words together) automatically means they can write a book.
4. Anyone who, no matter how well qualified they may be in other directions, has the humility to realise that they will need expert help to get their manuscript into a piece of first class book writing. In other words, you need an editor!

The only person who is right here is one who fits into the fourth category.

If you are in the first category, you now know that, no matter how badly you write, there are editors available to turn it into a first class piece of writing. And, if you don't want to go through the pain of writing it yourself, you can get a ghost writer to do it for you.

People who fit into the second or third category will never produce high quality work unless they change their attitude and put themselves into the fourth category.

The integrity of writing - a writer's responsibility to their readers

As a writer, you wield huge responsibility. Writers are held in awe by some people and in high esteem by others. There is a strongly-held assumption that having written a book somehow makes you intellectually superior. In one sense, this should be correct: if you write about something then you ought to know more about it than the 'common man'. The result is that people will form their opinions or make decisions based on what you write and it is completely irrelevant whether it is right or not - the effect on people's minds will be just as powerful as if it were. This is not only limited to non-fiction writers: two well-known writers who have abused their positions of responsibility are Dan Brown and Salman Rushdie, two writers who have made fortunes out of twisting the truth to appear as fact so successfully as to be believed by millions.

Fiction masquerading as truth is subversively dangerous. More overtly so are non-fiction works, especially those designed to teach or help people. The trouble is that a very large percentage of people who seek help from these books suspend their critical faculties and blindly follow dictates (if not diktats) that the most cursory view of what is actually happening will show up as false. Just one example: the whole personal development field from dieting to keep fit to personal relationships to success-attitudes is a minefield of books that not only lead people astray but all too often actually leave them in a worse state than when they started.

What this means is that you should carefully research the ideas you propose in your book. Your job is not to lead people astray, it is to educate them into what is right. We all have egos and, as a writer, you will find that you have to fight to avoid intellectual dishonesty in your work. As I said, people will swallow what you write whether it is right or wrong.

Writers are fond of hiding their misleading statements behind disclaimers on the fly page or, even worse, 'right to freedom of speech'. But any self-respecting writer should not consider this to be not a right, but a responsibility. What possible benefit to mankind is there in a right to write garbage?

How do I set about writing a book?"

Probably at least 99% (if not more) of books that are started are never completed. So this section is about the psychological aspects of writing a book, or how you go about making sure you are not one of the 99% who fail, and actually do end up getting your book into print. A splendid comment from a writer sums it up: "Nobody ever committed suicide while reading a good book, but many have while trying to write one."

Starting a book is easy, just as easy as setting off to run a marathon. But then, just like a marathon, writing a book becomes progressively harder and more tedious - if not more painful - the further you go. That is why so few budding authors who start out ever complete their work.

Just like trying to run a marathon, enthusiasm gets a book started. But the question is: "How do I keep going long after my initial enthusiasm has gone?" Especially when the realisation hits you that it is not the writing that is the problem; inspiration probably keeps that going nicely, and if that is all that was involved in being an author, many more books would be completed. No, it is the re-writing, the re-writing, the re-writing, the re-writing, the re-writing, that is the problem, when your manuscript is no more about inspiration but about craftsmanship, turning your inspiration into readable form.

Only about 1% of budding authors can get through this stage, and if you can see that you are rapidly approaching being one of the 99% of failures, it is at that stage you can save the day by employing an editor or a ghost writer, because you can give them your inspired jottings and leave it to them to turn it into a book.

I will be honest, no one can give you a sure-fire system (except turning your work over to an editor or ghost writer) that guarantees you will join the 1%. But at least I can give you some strategies to try.

The first and most important strategy is discipline

Writing a book is not a sprint, it's a marathon. If you try to write it in one big splurge, your book will inevitably end up badly written, and the ones that are hastily written are the ones that look as if they are a draft rather than a well-polished, finished article.

Like a marathon, book writing takes time and you won't complete it unless you pace your effort. Pacing means setting aside a part of each day, but no more than you can cope with day after day until your manuscript is completed. Pacing means little and often rather than big chunks of time occasionally: it is better to do one hour a day than eight hours on a Saturday. If you have plenty of time on your hands, of course you can set aside a lot of time daily. But many excellent books have been written on just one hour a day fitted around other jobs and commitments.

As to when you write each day, that will depend on your circumstances. If you can, the safest course is to make writing your first activity of the day, probably meaning that you will need to get up an hour or two earlier than you usually do. If you allocate your writing schedule for later in the day, you risk it being interrupted or postponed in response to distractions that may arise during the day.

But making writing your first task of the day will not work if you cannot manage the discipline of getting up earlier each day. In that case you could try making writing your last activity of the day.

Second, just get started!

The world is full of people who are going to write a book but never seem to get round to actually getting started. Delay actually means never. So what is wrong with getting started tomorrow morning? Don't put it off any longer.

Third, don't let anything interrupt your schedule!

First, be at your desk or computer ready to start work at the allotted time. Sometimes, the writing comes easily. At other times, it is a struggle. The temptation when the work is not coming easily is to give up for the day. That is not the way of the professional writer, who will sit there, even if writing nothing, until the allotted time is up. If your writing period is due to end at 8am, then you stay at your desk or computer until 8am.

Once you allow yourself to start later or finish earlier, it soon becomes an acceptable habit. Finishing a minute earlier may not sound like a problem, but once done, it soon becomes two minutes....then three, and, before you know where you are, your writing period has become shorter and shorter. Self-discipline again.

Other things that can interrupt your schedule, if you let them, are family, phone calls, emails. Your rule must be strict. Family and children are instructed that they must not interrupt you. Phone calls remain unanswered and emails unread. If you are writing at work, your staff must be under strict instructions not to interrupt you before your allotted writing time is over.

Learn to overcome your Magnets of Immediate Desire

To succeed in any endeavour, no matter what it is, you have to overcome nasty, evil little things called your Magnets of Immediate Desire, which will do everything they can to put you off, and in most instances, they succeed, which is why most people in life never achieve their dreams. The Law of the Magnets of Immediate Desire states:

"If a purpose requires disagreeable actions to be taken now, you will, unless you learn to fight it, find something else to do that is less disagreeable.

ALTERNATIVELY if there is a conflict between something you really DO want to do now, rather than whatever it is you ought to do to succeed, your immediate gratification will win."

As most writers work at home it is very easy to find excuses to interrupt your writing schedule. You may decide that you should do the ironing. Now, you hate ironing but even that is preferable to writing (that is what "finding something less disagreeable to do" means). If you are like most writers, you will frequently reach a point where you would rather do almost anything than writing. The question is whether you give in to that urge, or not.

Far more dangerous are the things you really want to do. If you are serious about writing then, at least until you have finished the manuscript, you may have to give up things you enjoy or which may be of great importance to you. It is easy to convince yourself that: "Why should I give up things that really matter to me?" or "I'm entitled to some time off", or "I've earned it." Not until you have finished your manuscript you haven't.

The temptations of things you really enjoy doing are far more difficult to resist, especially when friends or family are tempting you with, "You've been working really hard, so you've earned a little treat." That is why these are called 'Sugar-Coated' Magnets of Immediate Desire. The sugar hides the danger, but if you give in once, you will find yourself increasingly allowing your writing schedule to be interrupted.

Your This or That Card

This is a very effective in overcoming the Sugar-Coated Magnets of Immediate Desire. Get a 100 x 150 mm (4" x 6") index card or something similar and write on it:

> *"Would I rather do this*
> *or write my book?"*

Each time you get tempted by yourself or someone else to interrupt your writing schedule by doing something you want to do at the time, pull this out and read it. It works - or rather, if it does not, you should not be trying to write a book anyway.

Break down your work into Bite-Sized Chunks

What puts a lot of budding authors off is the magnitude of the task in front of them. This sometimes does not hit until you sit down to actually start writing, when the enormity of what needs to be done seems insurmountable.

The technicalities of how you layout, plan and prepare your book for writing, with skeletons, synopses, contents and points to be covered, are dealt with elsewhere in this book. Here I am concerned only with the psychology of how to make the insurmountable, surmountable. If I gave you the biggest apple I could find and asked you to stuff it whole into your mouth, you would not be able to do it. At least, it is rather unfortunate for you if you can. But if I cut it into small pieces, could you eat it then? That is what we call Bite-Sized Chunks, breaking the task into small, manageable pieces.

My philosophy of Bite-Sized Chunks is easy: Write a word. Then a sentence. Then a paragraph. Then more paragraphs. Pretty soon you will have a chapter. Then do the same until your book is finished.

Granny offers to help you dig the garden. Now, you're very fit but Granny can dig only with a trowel. Who will dig their half of the garden first? Obvious, isn't it?

But let's say that you hate gardening and keep giving up, as people often do in life, after turning a few spadefuls. Granny, however, keeps going with her little trowel for hour after hour at her own gentle pace. Who will finish the job first now?

The reason is that Granny has, more by luck than judgement, broken her task down to bite-sized chunks, chunks she can manage, whereas all you could see was a whole garden waiting to be dug.

I hate decorating. If I'm presented with a whole room to paint, I won't even start. But if I set a target of fifteen minutes' painting a day, even I can manage that easily - and it's remarkable how often, having started, I'll do a lot more than fifteen minutes.

Finally, don't set deadlines

Experienced writers can and do work to deadlines. They are often given deadlines by their publisher. Ghost writers frequently work to very tight deadlines. A book written by a retiring Prime Minister needs to be out as soon as possible after they leave office. If a well-known personality dies, the book of their life needs to hit the bookshelves as soon as possible after their death. A book about a traumatic event sells best as soon as possible after the event. But as a self-publisher and inexperienced writer, this does not apply to you unless there is a particular reason to get your book out as fast as possible.

Unless your book has to be finished by a certain date, setting a deadline is counterproductive. If you are ahead of schedule, it is all too easy to relax. If you are behind schedule, in your anxiety to catch up, your work is bound to suffer. Alternatively, some experienced writers set themselves a daily deadline of words to be written: "When I have done 4,000 words, I can stop." This again is not a good policy for you. Most writers can sit for hours without writing a word; at other times, the words come flooding out. Unless you are having to work to a deadline, the important thing is that your book gets written and ends up as polished as you can make it, not how long it takes. And if you stick to your daily schedule then your book will get finished, no matter how few or many words you write in each session.

David Barber

If you find it challenging to write, then be inspired by speaker, author and teacher Brian Mayne, creator of the world-leading achievement system Goal Mapping. Anthony Robbins said of him, "Brian is one of the best at helping people create a world-class blueprint for their life, not just goals but sustainable success. His Mapping Systems are a blast and really effective."

Learning from the School of Life
By international author and speaker Brian Mayne

"Who would have thought it?" These are the words that spring to my mind when looking back at my life and the many great changes I've seen in myself.

My name is Brian Mayne and I am an international speaker, author and coach, helping people to achieve their goals and dreams. My life now is so very different from what it was a few years ago.

I was born into a gypsy kind of life. My parents were travelling showmen who operated a funfair from place to place. The year I arrived into the world, my father decided that the fairground life was changing and becoming harder so he moved to the seaside, where he opened an amusement arcade on the Isle of Wight. Although he was quite successful right from the first season he missed the travelling life, and so, each year, we would have several different homes; one on the Isle of Wight for the summer season, one travelling around with the fair and a third home in Ashford, Middlesex where we would park up the funfair equipment for the worst weather months.

Along with these three different homes would come three different sets of friends and two, sometimes three or more, different schools each year. To say my education was poor is an understatement, it was absolutely destitute. Not that my parents were to blame. My mother in particular made great efforts and even employed a tutor to give me private lessons. Likewise, some of my teachers worked hard to try and help me learn, although there were many more that were happy for me to sit in a corner until it was time for me to move on again. Having said that, the real challenge was my dyslexia and, of course, the constant moving from home to home.

At 13 I dropped out of education and went to work full-time with my father. This may seem unusual but was actually normal for funfair people of my generation. Once I left school, what little reading and writing ability I had started to fade. By the time I was eighteen I couldn't even write a cheque, let alone fill out a form.

While I was quite embarrassed about it and hid the full extent of the problem even from my own family, I had a belief that I would be successful in life. At the age of 19, I became the youngest licensee in the UK when I took the family business in a new direction and, together with my brother George, opened a disco.

It was an instant success, going from strength to strength and becoming legendary for its alternative scene. For 10 great years, the business prospered and grew. Then in the recession of the late 1980s, as interest rates doubled and people's spending cash halved, it started to fall apart.

Over a two-year period, as the business slid into receivership, I lost what felt like everything in my life: my livelihood, my possessions, my home and even my marriage. I wound up a million pounds in debt, with no qualifications, no formal work experience and still relatively unable to read or write at nearly 30 years of age.

A Ray of Light

Although things looked bleak and I was, to be honest, frightfully scared, this was actually the beginnings of a bright new chapter in my life. In seeking to earn a little extra money I joined a network marketing organisation, and through it was introduced to the science of positive thinking and goal-setting.

I learnt how positive thoughts about ourselves, our lives or our current situation triggers the release of chemicals from our brain to give us positive feelings such as enthusiasm and confidence. The combination of positive thoughts and feelings creates positive attitudes which, in turn, empower us to take purposeful actions.

By setting compelling goals, we maintain and strengthen the positive brain cell connection and its release of feel-good chemicals that boost our motivation and command our subconscious to move us towards our desires.

The first meaningful goal I set was to learn to read and write well, and within a year I experienced the sheer delight as I achieved it. I felt so excited that at first I wanted to read everything. However, to honour what I saw as a great gift, I decided to focus my new reading skill on learning everything I could about personal development and self-improvement. As I applied the simple but powerful techniques of goal-setting and self-motivation, so my situation improved. I gradually repaid the debt, increased my results at work and created a bright new wonderful life.

A New Beginning

With each success and goal I achieved, increasing numbers of people wanted to know the secret of how I was able to turn my life around. I started making more and more presentations and discovered that people of any age and from any walk of life or occupation could also benefit from the techniques I had learnt. In 1995, I formed my own personal development organisation 'Lift International', which I set up with the purpose of sharing my life-changing systems of success with as many people as possible. The big ongoing goal I set for myself is to help lift seven million lives to a higher level of happiness.

As soon as I was clear on the goal, I started thinking deeply about how to achieve it. It quickly became obvious that it would take many lifetimes if I were to try and reach all seven million through running seminars and workshops. Increasingly I decided that publishing was a vital part of the answer, but I couldn't find a publisher who was interested in someone who had only recently learnt to read. So, in 2001 I self-published my first book, *Sam the Magic Genie*. It was a great success, selling out the first print run in just a few weeks.

If I had known how easy it was and how much benefit it would bring to people's lives, I would have done it much sooner. I now have three self-published books, another four in print with publishing houses, and I intend to self-publish many more in the near future. Together with my personal development CDs, DVDs, seminars and a new online programme, I have so far reached around one million people of my seven million target.

I now believe I will achieve my goal with increasing speed because technology is making it so much easier and more cost-effective to turn your knowledge and life experience into books and guides. And these can be easily distributed around the world using the many marvellous modes of modern communication. For the age in which we live 'knowledge' really is 'king'. However, turning your knowledge into a book is only one part of the process. Effectively getting it into the hands of other people is another, and requires successful marketing and distributions systems. I have heard many sad stories of self-published books going mouldy on garage floors because the author has no outlet to sell them. If we are to fully benefit from our knowledge, and help others do likewise, we must apply it with wisdom gained through life experience.

When I first discovered the power of positive thinking and learnt to read, I opened the floodgates of knowledge into my mind. I practised speed reading and would devour at least one book per week soaking up knowledge. Much of what I read was very new science that focused on the functioning of the brain and its impact on our mind. However, as I read more and more personal development material from around the world and written throughout the ages, I increasingly discovered that the principles of success have always been known. They are ancient, timeless and universal. They have been applied in every generation and by every individual who has ever achieved anything in any walk of life or endeavour.

Strangely, we are not taught these vitally important principles of success in our formal education so we have to learn them for ourselves. One day in my reading I encountered a proverb, "Be wise at speed. A fool at thirty is a fool indeed." It struck a cord with me and triggered an insight. Although I had learnt many of life's lessons by my 30th birthday, there were in truth many more that I was ignorant of or failing to apply, and I had therefore behaved in some foolish ways. Looking back, I can now see clearly how all the great calamities of my life could have been so easily avoided or quickly corrected if I had been aware of and applied the principles of success I now choose to live by.

The Key to Success

The principles that govern success are actually relatively few in number and simple in essence. Chief among them is the core principle that you become, attract and move towards whatever you focus on most. Your dominant and most often held thoughts, whether positive or negative, colour your perception, create your beliefs, alter your emotions and influence your actions, all of which contributes into shaping you, your life and its outcomes.

Successful people in any field focus on being successful. They think successful thoughts, which trigger a chain reaction of positive feelings and actions that invariably create successful results. Unsuccessful people, for whatever reason, do the opposite. They focus on lack, limitation and difficulty. Their mind is filled with all the reasons why they can't succeed. Their negative thoughts create limiting beliefs, de-motivation and ineffective actions.

Of course, very few people set out to be negative or create failure; it's simply that their mind focuses more on what they don't want, rather than on what they do want. And whatever we focus on becomes a goal or target for our subconscious autopilot to steer us towards. Most often negativity creeps in without a person even realising what is happening. Self-doubt and worry are the equivalent of negative goal setting. When we worry, we unwittingly start thinking over and over about failing, and our subconscious, not being able to make value judgements, simply takes our worries as targets to be achieved.

Learning how to set goals correctly is one of the master key to success because it helps you hold a positive picture of success in your mind, and thereby commands your subconscious to help you achieve it.

Goal Mapping is the world-leading success system that I created in 1995, and it has now helped around one million people turn their dreams into realities. My Seven Step System is a powerful combination of leading scientific breakthroughs balanced with ancient life principles which are designed to activate your whole brain and powerfully command your subconscious towards success.

Not only have I written best-selling books and CDs on the system, I have also created Goal Maps to help me be successful in all my publishing and authoring endeavours. It is without question the most powerful goal achievement system I have ever discovered anywhere in the world.

I always start any new book by creating a Goal Map, with the main goal being the finished book and the various qualities I desire for it. Once the book is completed, I create another Goal Map for the successful release and distribution of it. And I use a similar process for any writing project. It always works and I have recommended the process to many other authors.

If you would like to experience the power of the system and create your own Goal Map to assist you in your publishing success, go to www.goalmapping.com and check out our revolutionary, free, goal setting software.

Brian Mayne

Thank you Brian! Brian's excellent Goal Setting Tool is perfect for authors. Do visit his inspirational site, which is full of excellent ideas and strategies. www.liftinternational.com

So, before you read on, now is the time to go back over this section and to use it to give you clarity for your project.

- Do you now know what you know?
- Have you decided on the subject matter for your book?
- Where will you need to go to research it further?
- What is the big goal you want to achieve?
- What will writing a book help you to become?
- Who are you writing for?
- What is it they really need to know?
- How will you reach them?
- Have you explored this subject area on the web?
- What are people searching for?
- What are the most used keywords?

There may well be other questions that you have posed for yourself that you need to answer.

Before you can build a house, you need to put down firm foundations. Before starting your project, you need to have clarity of purpose, and a specific goal in mind.

It may be a long journey, but if you know where you are going, you can plan to get there one step at a time - provided you are walking in the right direction.

Another inspirational person is my next expert contributor, Jonathan Jay. There are few that can match Jonathan for his practical knowledge of marketing. His success is due to his Innovative style and also his focus. Here, he writes about niche marketing for authors.

The secret to making money from your books and information products

By Jonathan Jay, Chairman, NABO.
The National Association of Business Owners

There's a simple yet potent secret to creating books and information products that bring in more prospects, customers and profits but it's one that many writers seem unaware of.

They commit hours and hours to their book or information project and finally launch it and what happens? It bombs. They discover that the product they've invested so much time and energy carefully crafting is of little interest to the majority of people. In terms of return on investment (money, time and energy), it's a failure.

And that's because they've created a book or product without first finding out if there was a market for it.

They began their project with the belief that because they were interested in a particular subject that other people would be too. They thought their book or product would appeal to 'everyone'.

All too often it turns out that the finished product appeals to almost no one. That's because no one book can possibly be 'all things to all people'. The same principle applies to any product or service.

So, how do you ensure that your book or information product will be snapped up by prospects or customers the moment you've completed it?

What is the real secret to creating a book or information product that people actually want to buy and read?

You have to let go of the idea that your book or product should (or even could) appeal to 'everyone'. Instead of writing a book that you think will appeal to 'everyone in the world who knows how to read' narrow your focus... forget about producing a generic product and get specific.

The danger with being a generalist is that while it might give you a bigger market to aim your book or product at, it also brings with it greater competition. Rather than being a generalist become a specialist in one sector of the market and then when you've built up a readership or client base there, consider adding another sector. To create a successful book or information product, you must identify and target a particular group of people and then deliver exactly what they want. This is known as 'target' or 'niche' marketing - and it's what you must use for your project to be profitable.

The Chartered Institute of Marketing defines niche marketing as "The marketing of a product to a small and well-defined segment of the marketplace."

Contrary to popular opinion, narrowing your focus will actually result in more not less readers or clients. A good niche will give you between three and 10 times more clients than general or unfocused marketing. A good niche will also provide you with a long-term, sustainable advantage in your marketing that will position you apart from all the competition and attract an endless stream of prospects.

The key to finding a great niche is identifying where your passions and strengths allow you to package your product as a tangible solution to your target market's biggest unmet needs.

Peter Montoya, brand marketing specialist, says to target market effectively you must reject the 'all things to all people' model and narrow the scope of your prospecting.

"You must market your services to the people, companies and organisations that are likely to value your leading attribute. With consistent effort and quality tools, you can get most if not all of your business within this domain.

"Alas many independent professionals use the 'trawl net' method of marketing: they drag their net over a huge area and hope they catch someone - anyone. Sadly, casting a huge net takes a lot of money and the catch is usually bottom-feeders not trophy fish."

Being a specialist has another advantage - you are perceived as an expert in a particular field. Your specialism immediately confers a perceived degree of expertise.

By focusing on providing solutions to customers' problems, you'll be able to make a strong, targeted promise. The result? People will seek you out.

Establishing a niche helps make you and your products or services memorable, according to the 'Niche Doctor', Dr Lynda Falkenstein.

"A niche helps your potential customers find you and tell you apart from others with a good product."

She's found that many people are reluctant to focus on a small segment of a market for fear it will limit their opportunities and profits.

"They don't understand that small and narrow can be very deep. An effective niche focuses energy in one, positive direction. Building on your strengths always increases your chances of winning."

Writers often fear there may not be enough readers to go around. Fear is what keeps people out there floundering. The fact is that once you have defined your market you are much more able to focus on satisfying the needs of a specific group of people.

Without a niche you will be wearing too many hats as you try to satisfy all of the people all of the time. The danger is that you will burn out, become disillusioned and lose your focus. What you want to do is satisfy some of the people all of the time rather than all of the people some of the time.

"Niche marketing is the best kind of marketing of all. To find your next niche, just sub-divide your current niche."

Gary Bencivenga,
top direct mail copywriter

When you focus on a tightly identified niche, you can more effectively address the needs of that market and make offers that they are predisposed to take advantage of.

What's more, publishing to a target market carries less risk, less expense, is faster, and more likely to be profitable than publishing to just anybody, according to the author of Niche Publishing Gordon Burgett.

The trick to niche marketing is that the message is specific and highly targeted. It's extremely personal as in "I'm talking to YOU", personal and your content 'speaks' to the unique needs of your target. That's what makes it compelling.

Incidentally, you don't have to write for just one niche. But you must give each niche the feeling that this is all you do and you do it "especially for them."

Readers want to believe that your book or information product can truly fulfil their wants. If they believe you understand them, you meet their desires or if you've served somebody just like them, they will be more likely to try your book or product than the one that does not meet their specific wants.

To succeed in a big way, you need to find an underserved niche and provide information that people desperately want and need.

Note the word 'want'. There's a huge difference between 'want' and 'need'. People might know they 'need' to lose weight but won't feel motivated to buy your weight-loss book or product. If however they suddenly decide they 'want' to look better and to feel more energetic, they'll be more likely to buy your weight-loss book or product. People are motivated and compelled to take action because of wants rather than needs.

So your book or information product must address the wants (rather than needs) of your target audience. You must know the triggers or 'hot buttons' that will motivate them to buy.

Discover your niche

Follow these signposts to discover your niche:

1.　　Passion - It must interest you and be an area in which you already have some rapport, personal experience and enthusiasm. Consider your own talents, special interests and expertise, and aim your services towards others who share them.

2. Size - The niche must be big enough to supply you with as many readers as you need. Avoid choosing obscure or really miniscule groups (e.g. red-headed cave-dwelling hermits).

3. Money - The people in your niche must be able to afford your book or products.

4. Reach - You must be able to reach your clients easily through targeted promotions.

5. Contactable - You must be able to contact your readers by mail, through adverts, the Internet or even face to face.

6. Burning Need - Is there an intense, perceived need for the niche in the minds of your prospects? Are they truly concerned with the issue you can help them solve with your product or service? The more intense their pain or conversely, the more attractive the benefit you help them realise, the more quickly the niche will respond to your efforts.

7. Underserved - Is your niche underserved? One of the factors to consider is how many similar products or services are already being offered to the niche.

8. Precedent – Have other writers had success in this niche? If so, it suggests that people will pay to have a specific need addressed. You'll know that people with that need will be more responsive to marketing than if the niche had never been defined and addressed before. Some of the risk is reduced if you know that there are others that are successfully targeting the niche.

9. Being the first - Take a successful niche and narrow it further. For example, if your niche is aimed at first-time parents, you could be the first in your area to offer an additional product that you know they want.

10. Narrow focus - It's much better to offer your product or service to a narrow professional industry (divorce lawyers) than to a broad group (all lawyers).

11.   Industry focus - Are members of your niche from a single professional group or industry? If you focus on a subset of a specific professional group, the niche is much easier to penetrate. You can email a specific newsletter to your target group. You can market the niche through its local, national and even international professional organisations. You can forge alliances with suppliers who serve the same niche.

12.   Coherent group - It's a major advantage if members of your proposed niche feel they belong to a coherent group. Members are more likely to forward your promotional material to others if they know who the others are.

13.   Improved financial or performance benefits - Can you help your niche to make money or improve performance? While they're not essential criterion, it's easier for readers to justify buying your book if you're helping them to make more money or perform better professionally.

Research your niche

Interview at least three prospects to identify what their needs are, how best to communicate with the niche, learn more about the competition, how to quickly position yourself as an expert within the niche, and how best to package your product as the solution to the niche's greatest unmet, tangible needs that they are prepared to pay to resolve.

Test market your solution. Conduct a mini product or service launch to test the interest in the market and to obtain testimonials.

Roll out your finished product. Seek every opportunity to speak, write, present or share your knowledge with your target audience to increase your exposure and solidify your position as an expert solution provider to this niche. The greater the 'expert' profile you have with the group, the more responsive they will be to your invitation to do business with you.

Identify your specialty

Your specialty describes the benefit your product or service will offer your target market. With both your niche and specialty clearly defined and articulated, you are more likely to be perceived as credible and knowledgeable. All of your marketing materials, your articles, your books, products, workshops and public speeches should all be created with your target market in mind.

Testing your topic(s)

Once you select a target market about which you are knowledgeable and passionate (you can't succeed in any field unless you have passion for it), you can begin doing market tests

TIP - If there aren't any competitors in a niche market, don't get too excited. Usually no competition means you can't make a living with this target market. That's not a hard and fast rule...just a warning.

Writing Books People In Your Niche Will Buy

Once you've found a target market, you need a subject or topic to write about!

To find the right subject you have to discover what would motivate anyone within your target market to buy your book or information product.

You must identify the benefits that your book or information would provide. It must meet an overwhelming want or solve a major problem.

Focusing on the benefits helps people to understand why they should buy your book or product. It shows you're not like every other author - and that you're offering something special. It says you really understand your readers (customers) and what they actually want. The greater the want, the more likely people are to take action to meet it. And if the solution to that want is in your book or information product, the more likely it is that people will buy it. So you must identify that overwhelming want or massive challenge and then meet or solve it in your book.

You must provide eager buyers with information that is so crucial they won't think twice about buying it.

How do you identify an irresistible subject? The quickest and most effective way to find out what most interests your target market is to ask.

Survey your target audience and ask them what they most want to know about. Ask questions like "What are your three major challenges?" Do offer people an incentive to complete and return the survey.

Research the professional publications or trade journals, ezines and blogs they read to find out the hottest subjects. Find out about emerging trends in your target market. Search on Google to find other niche books about your topic. See what already exists (or soon will) among the books aimed at your market.

Pick the strongest subject (or combine two or three of the top subjects).

Once you've identified your target market, know what they want, how to reach them and how to convince them to buy your product, only then do you start writing.

Be aware that you don't have to be a leading expert in the world to write a book. You don't have to know everything in the world about your subject matter. You just have to know more than most people do about your subject. You need to know something that other people will want to know and you need to be able to organise what you write in a way that other people can follow. The information must be easy to understand and usable.

You don't even need to be the best writer in the world - in fact, you don't even need to be able to write. You can always hire someone to help you write your book. When published, the book will bear your name as the author. Or you can simply record your thoughts and have them transcribed then have someone else edit your transcripts into a book.

So now you know the secret of creating a book or information product that will sell - write on a subject that people within a defined target group are desperate to know about and willing to pay for. All you need to do now is take action!

Jonathan Jay
www.successtrackonline.com

"I don't have any yet. We just opened."

Part Two – Grow what you know

If, as part of your business life, you share your knowledge with staff, with customers, with suppliers, delivering training or as a platform presenter, every time you speak you are creating something of value. On that basis, you have probably written a number of books already if you were to count up the words you have generated. The bad news is that you didn't capture them in a form that enabled you to repurpose them later. What a waste!

They say that talk is cheap, but if you are an expert then every word you say has a monetary value. How much depends on how you use them. In my experience, most experts really enjoy talking and enthusing on their specialist subject, which is great. However, in doing so they tend to forget the value of the information they are generously giving away. If more value was given to these words, I guarantee that any expert would be earning much more than they may currently be doing.

For example, as an expert you may have delivered the same talk many times. You know more church halls and meeting venues than is safe to know. You are an old hand at working the audience. You get the laughs in the same places, you get the same questions at the end. You are a well oiled machine. In fact, when you get up in the middle of the night to get a drink and open the fridge door, when the light goes on you automatically do a 20 minute spot!

However, despite all of your polish, just now and again, someone will ask you a question from the back of the room that challenges you to dig deep down into your bank of knowledge and give the most comprehensive and illuminating answer you have ever given on the subject. As you walk back to the car with your slides and the bottle of undrinkable wine the organiser gave you, you hear yourself thinking, "If only I'd written that down." Too late. It is now lost for ever.

I firmly believe that any event that you speak at that you don't record in some form or another for yourself has cost you more money than you could ever have been paid for being there. Why? Because you will have lost the opportunity to use and repurpose that unique moment of creativity again in the future.

I maintain that, when you are a professional communicator, every word you speak in public has a monetary value. Open your mouth and Kerching! Another pound in your pocket. So how would you like to get paid more than once for just one live performance? It is perfectly possible. Here's how you can really leverage your time.

Say for the sake of argument, you are speaking to a group of 100 people. Each of them have paid ten pounds a head to hear you speak, and you do so for an hour. You have netted one thousand pounds at the door, ignoring any back of the room sales. Let's say you speak at the rate of 100 words per minute, for 60 minutes. Each word you spoke is worth 16 pence. Better than nothing, but it could be a lot better!

So, to leverage your time the next occasion you do this, you take a pocket digital audio recorder and a tie clip microphone and record the whole thing. Now, during the evening somebody at the back asked you a particularly good question which hits you at exactly the right moment. Straight off the cuff, you gave one of the most concise and inspired answer you have ever given in your life. Wow, you were good!

Now normally, what would happen is that you would come off stage and kick yourself saying, "If only I'd written that down." Well, this time, you don't need to kick yourself. Instead, when you get home you get the recording transcribed. Now you have a document which has captured you at your best. You now have some new options for these words, which if you remember, would normally only be worth 16p each. Now you can get additional value from them by using them as part of a workbook you could be selling at the back of the room. Kerching!

So what else can you now do? You could also repurpose your words as part of a magazine article. Kerching! Or even as a chapter in your next book. Kerching! Now don't forget that you have a good quality digital recording of your performance, so you can also take extract from it to use as part of an audio CD product. Kerching! Or even as a podcast for the members area of your website. Kerching!

Now, say that instead of simply recording the audio from your event, you had a video cameraman at the back of the room. This time you were on a radio mic and you were well lit on stage. Now you have some new opportunities. In addition to all the above, you could now use extracts from the event, with suitable introductions and links between sections to be recorded later, as the basis for a new DVD product. Kerching!

You can then repurpose some of the footage as a live stream on your website as a promotional tool to let potential clients see you at work. Kerching! Not only that, but you now have some material you could use as part of an online training course. Each module could include a streamed video clip. Kerching again!

So, what is the value of each of your original words now? Certainly more than 16p! Not only that, but you are going to get paid for them, time and time again in the future.

So as I said at the beginning, any event where you are speaking to a live audience, and don't capture it yourself in a way that enables you to repurpose it again and again in the future, has cost you far more than the original 16p per word that you would have earned before. Now do you believe me? So, what are you going to do about it?

Real cash in the attic

It might be that you are already sitting on a goldmine of old articles, speeches or workshops that are currently gathering dust. Don't think of it as boxes of old papers, think of it as your pension! If your greatest asset is your intellectual property, it can only realise its potential if it is in a form that you can easily use it and repurpose it.

If your material is currently only in paper form, then the first step would be to use an OCR (Optical Character Recognition) programme with a flatbed scanner to turn your material into a Word Document or similar. Now you have proper access to it again and can start extracting those nuggets of gold.

Scary movies

You might have some old videos of past lectures or training events that you have spoken at. Don't write these off as being no use just because they are in an old format and nobody has a VHS player anymore. Although the picture aspect ratio of flat screen televisions is 16:9 and your old video is the old TV size of 4:3, you could still use it as a streamed video in a small video window on your website. Because the image will be small, it will compress the image and the fact that it is not of the best quality will not matter.

Old material that is still relevant but just on an old format could have a new use as part of a video library on your website - possibly as a value-added part of a subscription based members area. Those video streams could also be used in online open learning modules which could be another way of making your I.P. accessible.

If the look of the video is too embarrassing to use - maybe you had hair then and don't now! Or it could be the kipper tie and the flairs that you can't live with - all is still not lost! You could still extract the audio from the programme and use it without the pictures. The audio quality, even with a little cleaning, would be ideal to include on an audio CD product, a podcast, or a simple audio file of the website.

But you still haven't run out of uses for your old videos yet. You could then take the audio files and get them transcribed into documents and then use the content to include in a book, a tips booklet, an article or a script. If the programme stands the test of time, you can always remake the video again, this time without the kipper tie!

The result of all this effort will be a pile of material to draw from.

One of the biggest challenges faced by authors is how to organise their research and their content. Without much help, a once tidy desk can become a mountain of paper, which is less than helpful when you are trying to clear your mind of clutter, and to get writing. One author has a big advantage of most. He is Phil Chambers, who, apart from running a very success company, Learning Technologies specialising in Mental Literacy techniques, is also the reigning Mind Mapping World Champion. Here are his thoughts on how to combine being an author with using Mind Maps.

Mind Mapping for Authors
By Phil Chambers

Starting to write can be a scary prospect. You are sure you have a lot to say but as you stare at the stark, blank white page of a Word document with nothing but a blinking cursor, you suddenly feel like a rabbit caught in car headlights. All creativity drains from your mind and is replaced by self-doubt. Where do I begin? How do I construct a cogent, well-argued and structured masterpiece and not a rambling mess?

You need an intermediate step between your mind and the written words. An easy way of getting your ideas down in a far more friendly environment. This conduit between your mind and the page is a Mind Map - a tool originated by British psychologist Tony Buzan in the early seventies. Don't worry that it's 40 years old. It has stood the test of time because it works.

Start by drawing a picture in the middle of the page (or just choosing one if you are using Mind Mapping software).

Your page is no longer blank. It's friendlier already. Add curved, flowing branches radiating out from the centre, each in a different colour. Place a single word or image on each line that sums up your ideas and then sub-branches (or twigs) off the end of these to develop the ideas.

Each main branch is a category of thinking, sometimes called a Basic Ordering Idea (BOI). Try not to have too many BOIs - between seven and 10 tend to work best but there is no limit on the number of twigs or how many levels you can go down. Don't use sentences. Don't judge your ideas. Don't worry about structure or correct spelling. All this can come later. The aim is to get your creative juices flowing and capture everything.

When you get into the right frame of mind with a torrent of ideas coming thick and fast, typing or even scribbled notes can't keep up. Mind Maps can! Because you are only adding single words you have far less to write to record everything. If you use iMind Map software, there is a great feature called Speed Mind Mapping Mode that allows you to type and add new branches with a single keystroke. It takes care of the process so you can concentrate on the content.

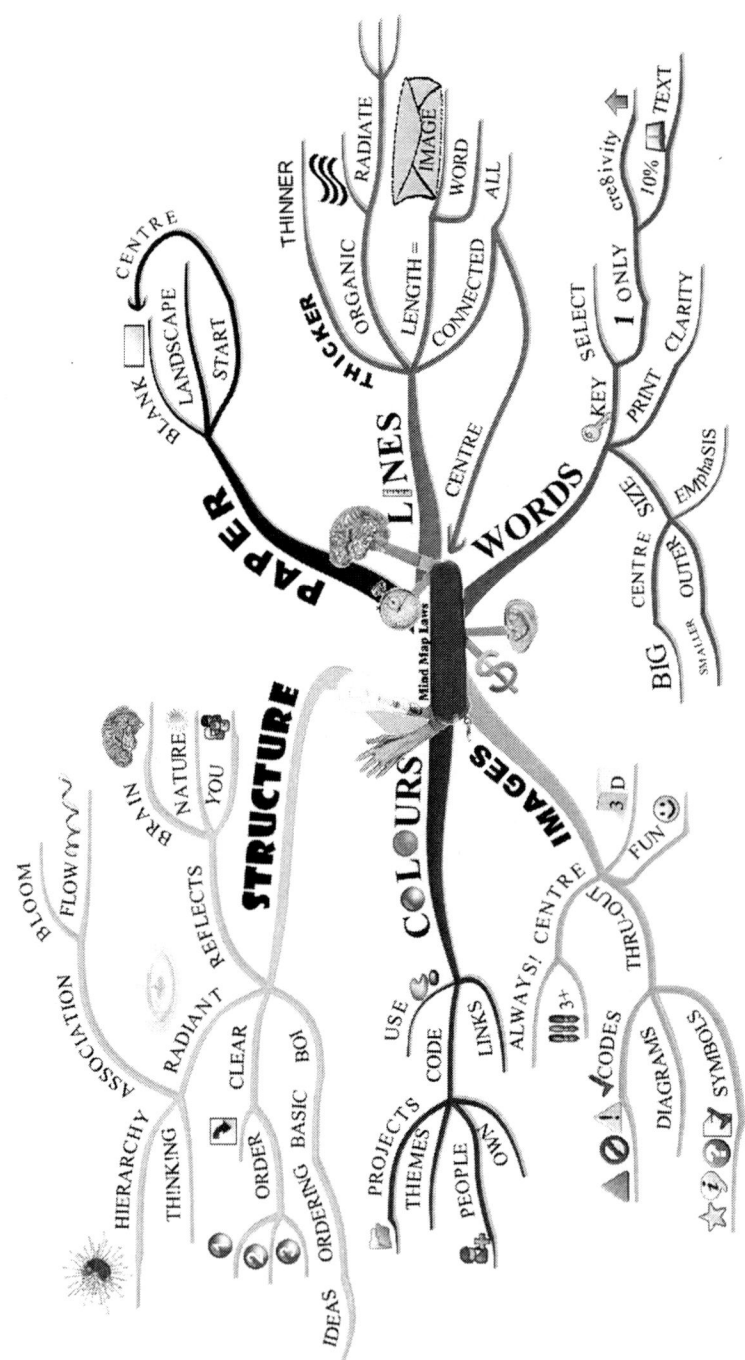

If you have the opposite problem of too few ideas or just run out of steam, add a number of blank branches. Your brain hates incompleteness and will come up with as many ideas as you have spaces to fill. Writer's block becomes a thing of the past.

Getting your ideas down is only the beginning. You need a structure for your book to organise everything and identify any gaps in your knowledge. Mind Maps help you here too. In exactly the same way as before, create a branch for each chapter based on your first Map. Transfer ideas onto the structured Mind Map adding them where they fit, editing as you go. There will probably be things that don't fit so ignore them or add ideas that they trigger that do fit. If you find there are areas on the Mind Map that you don't have enough information to develop you can quickly identify what needs to be researched.

How do you collect and combine ideas from various sources? Use a Mind Map! Are you beginning to see a pattern here? The central image in this case represents the topic or question that you need to answer. Add keywords on branches from Googled web pages, relevant books, articles, etc. In the software you can even add links to documents or web pages.

The beauty of having a Mind Map outline for the whole book is that you can see the wood for the trees. You don't have to start at chapter one and keep going till you reach the end. Start with the chapter that you feel most comfortable with. Because the structure is already in place, it will all fit together like a jigsaw. The harder chapters can be written when you get into your stride. Use a highlighter pen to strike off each part as it is written. This keeps you motivated, gives you an immediate visual indication of what you have achieved and shows you which bits remain.

Having this continual monitoring process keeps you on track and helps you to better manage your time. Another benefit of having the whole book mapped out in advance is that it greatly reduces the need to redraft or edit what you have written. Because the processes of thinking and writing have been separated, both are clearer.

If you create beautiful Mind Maps with lots of images, you can use them to illustrate the book. Add your whole-book Mind Map next to the contents page. Alternatively, every chapter can open with a Mind Map that prepares the reader for what is to come. They will get a lot more from the book by understanding the framework and context first.

As this book shows you, writing is only the beginning. You have to market it effectively. Mind Maps can be used as presentation frameworks. Because of their visual nature you can easily remember the content after a few reviews. This allows you to present confidently and in a more engaging manner without the need for notes.

Once you get used to using Mind Maps, they become a natural way of thinking and you use them automatically and almost unconsciously. You'll wonder how you ever managed without them!

Phil Chambers

Organising your thoughts on a Mind Map is one thing. Organising your desk, and workspace is another - especially if it is in the "eye of the storm" that most of us live in.

Author Rachael Ross has recently published an invaluable book for authors, and indeed anyone who is running a business from home. It is called *How to Make Working From Home Work For You* (Published Filament Publishing 2010 £10).

Rachael, of Purely Peppermint, provides specialist consultancy services in developing and introducing an effective home working environment. She works with individuals and businesses by providing bespoke practical solutions for their home office. Through leadership, training, hands-on and telephone support and advice, Rachael ensures that her clients have the greatest of success in their chosen field. To help achieve that success she instructs on setting boundaries, dealing with isolation, managing clients, managing your time, finding work/life balance, plus much, much more.

A regular contributor to leading working from home websites and magazines, Rachael was invited to the Home Business Summit at the House of Commons to advise central government on how to improve and support home businesses.

Rachael is focused on her clients achieving productive and effective results. Her continual commitment can be seen through the monthly newsletter, packed full of practical tips and solutions to all your home office troubles. For more information on Purely Peppermint and a chance to sign up to her excellent newsletter, please visit www.purelypeppermint.com

Working From Home Guide For Authors

By Rachael Ross of purelypeppermint.com

Since childhood you may have filled every spare moment writing short stories and dreamt of one day writing a book. That moment is here, now that you have decided to take the plunge. There aren't many careers more perfectly suited to working from home than being a writer. It may be perfectly suited, but you still need to establish an effective working environment and I would recommend starting with these three areas.

1. Home office

This is where all the action is going to be taking place and great master pieces will be written. So you want your office to allow you to work as effectively and successfully as possible. The ideal would be to have a separate room designated as your office. But if that is not possible, you need to create a designated office space, somewhere quiet and with a little bit of privacy.

For a writer, your office should include:

- An ergonomic chair
- A work station with enough room that allows the keyboard to be at the right height and avoid straining your wrists
- Computer positioned at the correct height to avoid neck strain
- Printer
- Filing storage for paperwork
- Shelves to store larger items like office supplies or reference manuals

- Sufficient lighting
- An inspiring photo, saying or painting

This is a room where you are going to be spending many hours in. So there is no better time to start taking advantage of the benefits you will enjoy while working from home and create an office space especially suited to all your needs.

2. Distractions

Home is a comfortable place to be and there are many distractions that could get your attention. Imaging you are sitting at the computer ready to start writing when out of the corner of your eye you spot a pile of ironing and the desire to deal with that almost takes over. Or a friend who is on holiday calls because they know you are only working from home, so not really working (or so they think). They wanted to ask you out for lunch. Of course, that would be nice but you have a deadline...so what do you say?

How to deal with distractions:

Household - There will be many chores you could take care of on any given work day, but you have to decide what tasks are going to be allowed. Washing up your lunch dishes may be ok, but deciding to give the oven a quick clean is not.

Computer - As a writer, your computer is everything. The tool to your trade, but also a potential distraction and a way of avoiding work. Turn off the email auto reminder and only look at your emails at set times throughout the day. Also turn off anything else in your office that will not allow you to work with a clear mind.

Friends and family - There is still a misunderstanding regarding the idea of working from home and because of that, friends and family may end up being a distraction. From the outset let everyone know what your office hours are, and how best to contact you within that time. If you are going to be working when family is around, try placing a simple sign like 'I'm Working' on your desk or the door of the office. This will help to remove some of the uncertainty regarding whether it is a good time to interrupt and talk to you

3. Create a schedule

There can be so much flexibility in a schedule when you are based at home. On the plus side, a schedule can be created to fit around your family and any responsibilities you may have. On the downside if the flexibility gets the better of you, you may end up frittering the day away and not writing a single word. What you need to create is focus and creating a schedule for the day will help to give you that focus. Don't get stuck in the trap of thinking that there is a typical home office schedule. There is no such thing and it is certainly not the traditional typical office hours of nine to five.

When you create your schedule, consider:

- Do you need to take the children to school?
- Are you fitting this around another job?
- What else do you need to fit into your day?
- What other responsibilities do you have?
- When will your home be the quietest and allow you to work uninterrupted?
- Do you have more energy and work better in the morning?
- Does your energy pick up early afternoon till late in the evening?

There are two thought patterns regarding an ideal schedule. First it is recommended that you start at the same time every day, having a regular routine. The second one is for your schedule to be a bit more fluid. I feel it doesn't matter which one you go for, as each have positive aspects that will suit different types of individuals. The most important part of a schedule is to create one and use it.

I completely enjoy the flexibility working from home gives me. At the start of the week I look at my schedule which is usually divided between working at a client's home helping them master the skills needed to successfully work from home, to being in my home office taking care of all the other work tasks related to running a business. The days I am with clients are blocked off, but on the other days I create a schedule to suit me best which is usually starting a bit later in the morning till early evening. If there is an exhibition I want to see, I schedule that on a weekday (when it is usually quieter in London) and schedule the work day on the weekend. For me, this is a near perfect schedule.

From day one of working from home, you want to create a schedule to make the best use of your time and accomplish more.

This is only the tip of the iceberg when it comes to successfully working from home, but I have given you a place to start. In my book *How to Make Working From Home Work For You*, I cover everything you need to know about working from home effectively. The book is available at www.purelypeppermint.com and if you order now you will receive a bonus report on the 10 mistakes made when working from home.

Rachael Ross

Wise words, Rachael. Thank you!

As an expert, no matter what field you are in, you will need to keep and refer to a large body of material on your specialist subject for articles, books and speeches. Unless you can find your way through all of this information easily, you will find it very difficult to function effectively.

If you are on top of your subject, then new information will be arriving every day. Trade journals, press cuttings, correspondence, catalogues, programmes, minutes, reports - the list goes on and on. The challenge is going to be creating a system that will allow you to find what you need quickly and to know where everything is.

When you have a river of paper running through the house, it doesn't take long for it to become a flood. So if you are currently drowning, there is a simple solution - and it doesn't involve a box of matches! All you need is a simple, predictable system that both you and anyone else who is supporting you in your efforts can easily understand and implement.

The trouble about tidying and filing old papers is that you will be tempted to sit and read each piece of paper and every article you come across. After all, it is your life's work you are reviewing. Well, resist the temptation; remember nostalgia isn't what it used to be.

The Golden Rule is, when you are going through archive material, you must adopt the "One Touch" principle. Once you pick something up you need to put it into its new permanent home, not in another pile! Applying this rule may well save your sanity and also dramatically shorten the time that this takes.

Firstly you will need to have a filing system. This might involve a filing cabinet, although it is not an essential. You might use box files, folders, lever arch files or large envelopes, wallets, or plastic pockets. It doesn't matter what system, as long as there is a system.

Next you need a 'Key'. This is one sheet of paper that lists all the categories that you will be putting your documents in. The simplest of these is known as a Decimal Filing System. There was a time in my life when my desk was piled high with stacks of papers and I could find nothing. I was introduced to this simple system and one day later, not only did I have a tidy desk, but I could find everything with ease. It probably added years to my life. The most difficult thing is starting, but once you do it will make a massive difference.

The key to a decimal filing system is to create 10 main categories. If you were running a business, your categories might be -

100	Property
200	Suppliers
300	Staff
400	Accounting
500	Customers
600	Advertising
700	Market Research
800	Trade Associations
900	Travel

As you pick up a piece of paper, you would decide which of these main categories it fitted within and then open a sub-category for it. For example, a letter about repairs to the roof would go into Section 100 Property and may go into a new sub-category 101 Repairs. 102 might be Utilities, 103 might be Buildings Insurance, etc. With 100 sub-categories in each section, you are unlikely to run out of options.

In the future when a piece of paper presents itself, simply refer to the master list of categories and select the most appropriate. Using this system, you will always be able to find everything and still keep a stress-free, tidy desk. The good thing is that you can share a copy of the master list with your helpers and know that they will be able to follow it as well.

Now you have easy access to your potential fortune. More importantly, you no longer have the excuse that you can't find anything (sorry!).

Your New Best Friend

Computer engineers inhabit a world of their own which has its own language and sense of humour. The latest acronym to emanate from them is P.I.C.N.I.C - which apparently stands for Problem In Chair Not In Computer.

Another helpful acronym in Geekland is usually the correct answer to most problems. And is simply the initials, 'R.T.F.M' which, when translated means, 'When all else fails, and as a last resort - Read The F****** Manual'!

Whether or not when you unpacked your computer for the first time you thought the mouse was a foot pedal is not the point. The point is that, if you are to be successful as a professional communicator, you need to change your mindset about the relationship you have with your PC.

For most people their PC is a Swiss Army Knife of all possible solutions. It is their email provider, their games console, their social networking window, their Internet browser, their YouTube viewer, and numerous other things beside. However, as an author it is just one thing. The most important tool you have for your business.

No matter what profession you are in, the tools of one's trade are treated with respect. A tree surgeon would never work with a blunt axe nor a dentist with a blunt drill (I hope!). Nor should you trust your project to any machine that you don't have total faith in or control over.

We service our cars regularly because we take our safety very seriously. The majority of people don't give the same level of care to their PCs and as a result, they can prove to be unreliable. When your writing and your research are so precious, you cannot afford to entrust them to anything that could let you down. There are too many stories of hard drives failing, or viruses deleting data not to take this seriously.

Have you ever wondered why so many businesses forbid their employees to surf the web during office hours? It is because of the danger of inadvertently downloading malicious software. And there are lots out there!

There are two protections you must have in place:

Virus and spyware protection. If you are not a computer buff, get proper advice on this because no one system will protect you from all possible attack. Professionals may have three or more systems in place to catch the nasty blighters.

Back up your material at least once a day. If you are working all day then you should also do this at lunchtime (or if you are a typical mad writer working all night, then at midnight!).

So if you are working from home on a PC that is shared by the rest of the family, you have a number of potential problems:

- Getting access to it when you need to
- Ensuring that it remains a safe and robust environment
- Avoiding someone else downloading something potentially dangerous
- Keeping your data secure

These days, with the cost of notebook computers and laptops coming down in price, a good solution is to have a machine of your own that can be totally dedicated to your project. It is a business expense after all, and deductible for your tax.

Having a dedicated machine means:

- You can keep it uncluttered of distracting non-business application
- As your family will be able to use the main PC, they will give you peace to work, rather than pestering you to check their Facebook account
- You can move your workstation to a peaceful and calm location at any time
- You can be certain that nobody else will have downloaded anything that might compromise security
- You can keep your hard drive defragmented regularly and virus scans up to date
- And most of all, you can back up your data onto a memory stick after every session so your project is never at the mercy of your machine.

Your Support Team

As we said, writing is a lonely profession. Some writers can cope with this and don't rely on anyone but themselves. However, others can't handle it without a support team consisting of people to bounce ideas off or who can provide help, support or encouragement. You may also need to find people with the technical skills you don't have.

For example, if you don't type particularly well it might help to find someone who can. This doesn't have to cost money. I am a great believer in the concept of Soft Money. You might trade babysitting with someone who happens to be a great audio typist. Be creative! What could you do for someone in return for them doing what you need? The concept of bartering is alive and well!

Preparing yourself for action

This covers two areas:

- Getting your head round working from home
- Creating a success-attitude

Working from home

Many new writers have never worked from home before. If you are one of them, it can come as quite a culture shock. So let's prepare you for these. Most problems come under the following headings:

- Family adjustment
- Work-initiation
- Loneliness of working on your own
- Insecurity of income

- Taking sole responsibility
- Self-discipline with no 'bosses'.

You will also learn a big difference between people who succeed and those who don't - their attitude to work.

The problem of family adjustment

We dealt with this earlier. It isn't only you who will have to adjust. Your family will as well.

The problem of work-initiation

People in the workplace rarely have to look for work because it's piled up in front of them. Even managing directors spend more time responding to work landing on their desk than on work created or initiated by themselves. But when you start working from home, it's down to you to find and initiate the work. And it's quite simple; if you don't initiate it, nothing will happen. This can be tough.

The problem of loneliness

If you have been used to being surrounded by people at work, part of a team and working communally, working from home all by yourself can be a lonely experience and it can take getting used to. You may think you are surrounded by family. No, you're not because you will have told them to keep away during your working hours, so if everyone is carrying out their part of the bargain, your family might as well be a million miles away...

The problem of income insecurity

Some people take a while to adjust - if they adjust at all - to not having the cushion of wages or a salary coming in. If you've spent your whole life being programmed to know that you get your pay-packet whatever you do, it can be very difficult to get your head around the fact that, from now, no money is going to come in unless you make it.

The problem of sole responsibility

For most people, until they start working from home, all the decisions they made at work will have been made with other people. If anything went wrong, the load of responsibility would have been spread, and it is a great relief to be able to share the pressure when things go wrong. There is huge comfort in having a gang around you.

But when you start working from home, there is no gang, there is no mutual support. There is no one to share responsibility with. From now on, it's down to you and you alone. If you make a mistake, it is entirely yours and no one else's. Some people find that tough to deal with.

The problem of self-discipline

In an office or factory, you don't need much self-discipline to keep your personal matters out of work time. Do the work you are supposed to do, follow company procedures and ensure your work is up to standard, because you'll get fired if you don't. But when people work from home, there isn't anyone to make them stick to good working practices and many of them find they don't have the self-discipline needed.

The same applies to the time disciplines of work. In an office or a factory, if you don't get to work on time, if you take more breaks than allowed or if you finish early, you stand to get fired. But at home, with no one to make you, it can take great self-discipline to stick to good time-keeping.

Where your activities are concerned, the stark reality is that everything you do related to getting your book completed will get you closer to achieving that, whereas everything you do that is not related to getting your book completed not only won't do that - it will actually take you further away from your goal, making it less likely that your book will ever get published. Therefore, the philosophy behind working from home should be quite simple: concentrate on the first and avoid the second.

To succeed in any endeavour, no matter what it is, you have to overcome those nasty, evil little Magnets of Immediate Desire which will do everything they can to put you off, and in most instances, they succeed, which is why most people in life never achieve their dreams. If you are like most writers, you will frequently reach a point where you would rather do almost anything than write. The question is whether you give in to that urge, or not.

Related to the above is that people worry far too much about their likes and dislikes, so they favour what they like doing to the disadvantage of what they dislike doing. They select their priorities according to what they like and they spend as little time as they can on doing tasks they dislike - if not avoiding them entirely. A hallmark of people who succeed in getting their books published is that they don't let likes and dislikes get in the way. They select priorities strictly according to what needs to be done and they give each task the time it needs irrespective of whether they enjoy it or not.

How do we overcome the Magnets of Immediate Desire?

1. You create a schedule

If you are going to be writing full-time, the solution is easy: a full-time job requires full-time hours. The big luxury is that, as you are working from home, you can set your own. In that case, start from the time of day (or night!) when you are most productive and creative, and then compromise that in any ways that are absolutely essential to fit in with family demands. Notice 'absolutely essential' there. Compromise always means that you will be working at times when you are less productive and creative.

If you will be writing part-time, this usually means either having to fit your writing time around other commitments. So when you write each day will depend on your personal circumstances.

As a rule of thumb, the safest course is to make writing your first activity of the day, probably meaning that you will need to get up an hour or two earlier than you normally do. If you allocate your writing schedule for later in the day, you risk it being interrupted or postponed in response to either distractions or false ones (Magnets of immediate Desire) that may arise during the day.

Some people have such a flexible job that they don't know from one week to the next where they are going to be. In that case, a fixed writing schedule obviously won't work, and you may have to, for example, work out your writing schedule at the beginning of each week for that week. In that case, block out the times you will devote to writing in your diary otherwise it won't get done. Our experience, however, is that people who work to a week-by-week schedule are more likely to give up writing than those who have a permanent weekly schedule. But if that is the only way you can work a schedule then you must do it, but be aware that you will need more discipline.

2. Don't let anything interrupt your schedule!

This is self-discipline - possibly the vital requirement - for working at home. Let's accept that you may have a job that demands a last minute change in your writing schedule. Let's also accept that a genuine situation may crop up that must take precedence over writing time. First make sure the interruption is not Magnet of Immediate Desire, a convenient excuse not to write. If it isn't, if you have a success-attitude, then you will try very hard to make up the lost hours during that week.

That apart:

> *"I write when I'm inspired, and I see to it that I am inspired at nine o'clock every morning"* (Peter DeVries)

> *"I never could have done what I have done without the habits of punctuality, order, and diligence, without the determination to concentrate myself on one subject at a time"* (Charles Dickens)

Getting down to writing

To start this section, I have invited author and playwright Colin Bennett to share his thoughts about writing. Colin is a multi-talented individual and simply listing his achievements doesn't do justice to him.

Colin Bennett is a RADA trained actor, perhaps most famous for his role as Mr Bennett, the accident prone caretaker and straightman for Tony Hart in the BBC children's programmes *Take Hart* (1977-1983) and *Hartbeat* (1984-1989). He also portrayed the father in the 1985 Yellow Pages/Hornby advert *Signal Box*.

Amongst other TV duties, he presented *Night Shift* and *You Should Be So Lucky*, as well as appearing in *The Hitchhiker's Guide to the Galaxy* as Zarquon. He wrote a couple of TV series including *Captain Zep - Space Detective* and *Luna* before moving into the production field. He has a background in acting in and directing plays, notably appearing in and directing the musical version of *The Point!*.

Colin runs his own production company, An Acquired Taste TV Corp, and has been making broadcast television for about 17 years. Its name reflects its aim to be an 'Acquired Taste' in that they have specialised in slightly edgy products and the notion of 'acquired content'.

I am sure you will enjoy Colin's quirky style of writing in his article.

Writing not Wronging!
By Colin Bennett

My favourite writing quote is from the great but seldom performed stage play by John Van Druten called *I Remember Mamma*. It tells the story of a small town girl in the States who wants to be a writer. Her mother takes her to see a book signing by a visiting famous authoress to ask what the daughter should do. The famous writer asks, "Does she want to be a writer, or does she write?"

This is brilliant, particularly associated with the writing genre. The fact is that no one is out there telling you NOT to write! Even the despicable Marquis de Sade, who was forbidden to write his obscene accounts of depravity, was able to fill 600 pages of sickening descriptions while locked up in the Bastille, even though he was starved of ink and paper! Sorry to have made this sound so interesting. The work isn't.

Ironically, he wrote it on toilet paper. Flick through a few pages if you like but don't buy the books and please don't waste your brain reading it all. The point is, he wanted to write and though no one else wanted him to, he did.

The same can be said of us all. The major and most fundamental block to any of us writing is simply not doing it! I'll try, if I can, to cover various kinds of writing, though as I scan the shelves of my study noticing Shakespeare, Wilde, Poe, Conan Doyle, Dickens and thousands of others, I'd better be absolutely honest with you and say that I don't consider myself a real writer. I write. I wouldn't want to sully the name of the many people whose work I admire by pretending to be in the same league. I have written a great deal and have sold most of it, or been commissioned to write it. The trick of it simply hides in being able to do it, not judge it.

I think I'll begin with, though it could be anywhere, the writing that you SHOULD do!

'Writing for Posterity'. I don't mean massive literary tombs over which scholars will pontificate for the next 200 years. You can forget that or leave it in a drawer, for all I care. I mean the writing which you are under the most obligation to write and which, happily, fits into the most used criteria for writing at all.

Most writers, or critics, will often give the first rule for writing being "Write what you know best." Good rule. If you think I have anything to offer you then the chances are that you are at the beginning of your writing career. So I believe the rule as well. But much more fundamentally than that... Why do I think that you are under an obligation to write?

I have spent several years trying to find the details of my ancestors. I haven't done badly and some of my family have done much better. We have dates of births and deaths, marriages and some occupations and a few unknown middle names along with a few names we never knew before. What we don't have is anything else! Who were they? What did they think? What world did they live in? What rules did they live their lives by? What did they wear, eat, believe?

Now I have a page of places, dates and names, what the heck does it tell me about the people? I would give a great deal to have a few pages written by my maternal great Grandmother about her possibly apocryphal but much quoted encounter with Jack the Ripper. Such a letter doesn't exist. Who'd have thought? The only letter I have about her, extracted from the old family safe around which so many family stories centre, is a letter from a neighbour saying that my great Grandmother should be put into the workhouse because she is becoming so difficult to live near! This is not the same woman who lived for so long in the East End of London and was a local celebrity with her fox furs and liquor licence. Where is that woman? Long lost and forgotten as one day I will be.

So my first serious writing exercise, and I believe it should be yours too, was to put on paper every story that my (your) mother and father ever told me about their childhoods or parents or youthful exuberance. One day, hopefully before I get too old to remember and before the neighbours say I should be moved to the workhouse, I'll write my own stories of my own childhood, youth and life's work. But at least now my parents' chapters are already written. They will never be published, though in this age of digital printing I might get a few dozen printed off for distribution to the extended family. I will at least have something in a drawer somewhere for my great grandchildren to find and hopefully pour over for a few minutes when I'm long gone to answer all the questions that require something more than my date of birth and my date of death and those of my forebears.

Bearing in mind that I hope to get you to write more, I'd better start by giving you some advice about how to start this enterprise. First... Just blooming do it! This is not going to be a best seller. This is not going to win the Pulitzer Prize. This is just practice. And you can't practice without writing. And you can't write without a need. So your first mission, if you are prepared to accept it, is to write down everything you know. I accept that you might have something more pressing to write that is required to be delivered by next Friday. In that case, you might have picked up my humble work too late. Just get your head down and tap your little fingers off and come back to me once the work is delivered and paid for. Best of luck! Practice, practice, practice. But where to start?

Chronology is a great short cut to planning. I'm not good at dates or places or even planning, but I can remember what my father told me his first memories as a child were. That's where I'd start. And while I think that planning is a good idea, even an essential idea in a murder mystery or a text book, don't ever waste time planning when you could be writing. Words on a page are the golden part of writing. Planning is the distraction that might prevent you writing a single word. Are you still writing on a typewriter? Are you still writing with a fountain pen? Give it up unless you are famous for it. Word processing is the tool by which we can all aspire to being Jeffrey Archer. The words can be changed and changed until they are correct and the story is perfect or, in Jeffrey Archer's case, sold in their millions.

Staring at a blank screen is not writing. In fact, it is called 'staring at a black screen'. Writing is where you place words on a page. They might be good words, bad words, wrongly ordered words, brilliantly cogent words or a pile of nonsense words... But once they are down on paper or on screen they can be words re-arranged into ANYTHING. And if you want to take 20 years to make that order perfect, then you take it, that's your privilege. But until you have a few words in the wrong order, what will you correct?

What will you spend your time doing? Thinking? Getting it right first time? Why? You might never get it right first time, second time, third time, ever. So get over it. Get it down.

Move on and finish the pile of illogical, irrational, badly constructed, badly spelt, badly tensed, ill-formed thoughts. Time enough, when the last full stop has gone down, to take a breath, drink tea and go back to the beginning and get it righter, or wronger, but closer to what you thought you wanted to write.

Don't be surprised that it isn't anything like the work you wanted to write. The work writes itself. Honestly. Mind you, only if you actually do it. The muses take over if you let them. And in my humble opinion you should let them.

So what if it isn't the book or play or biography that you meant to write? No one was even expecting you to stop drinking long enough to finish the first page. But now, here it is, 200 pages of something. Ignore this section if you can't finish the first page and get on with just writing something. Don't give us excuses, we can all write those! Give us words. I have always had a facility for hard work. I'm not literate, good at spelling, good at story telling, good at sentence construction. I am hopeless at all those things, and many more. But I can focus. How do you imagine Dickens got all those words scratched into paper, time after time, after time? I have no idea, but I imagine that once he was told that he had two days to get the next instalment onto his publisher's desk or he wouldn't get the next instalment of the fee, he got on with it!

For the moment I'm going to ignore the 'planning' kind of writing. Not because I don't approve of it or don't want you to get used to planning but simply I don't want you to get bogged down with learning 'the scales' when you could be learning to play 'Claire de Lune'. It's a fairly easy piece to play on the piano, up to the bit where it gets difficult, but you can learn to play it without knowing any scales. I had rather you got on with writing than wasting your time assuming you will need high powered professional tools as required by a concert pianist, which, for the moment I'm presuming you will never be, sorry. So, without any preparation at all, just write. The chances that this will be a prize winning piece of work are slim and if it is, there will be plenty of people telling you where you went wrong. So another major rule: Let other people tell you where you went wrong, don't waste any time doing it yourself. You are not qualified. Leave it to the clever dicks. For the moment, your only objective is to write, write long and hard, write good and strong but write.

How? I am faced with a black screen and my mind won't write anything. Don't be pathetic. Write something, we are only practicing. It would be interesting to know how many pieces of work start with the words, "I'm sitting in front of a blank sheet of paper and I simply can't think of anything to write..." If that's all you write today, that's enough. Don't cross it out, don't start again, don't abandon the work, don't chuck it out with the baby. You have to learn to let go. I could write

a thousand sentences that could easily be the next sentence. They would be appropriate, or not, exciting, or not, stupid, or not. I'll bore you with a few just to prove it. "I'm sitting in front of a blank sheet of paper and I simply can't think of anything to write...

I may never write another word because I'm so boring." Or "I'm sitting in front of a blank sheet of paper and I simply can't think of anything to write. My mind keeps going back to the man on the beach. Who was he? Why did he stand there looking up at the old house on the bluff?" Or "I'm sitting in front of a blank sheet of paper and I simply can't think of anything to write.

Is it because my intellect won't allow me to write something stupid? Am I stopping myself from writing my novel just because I know my brother will make fun of it. I know already that it will be badly spelt." I know. None of these sentences are the start of a major work of literature. Forgive me, but they caused me no pain. AND you and I know that I could think of a thousand other sentences that could appropriately follow each of the ones I bothered to place on the paper or screen. So while each of those examples could be the first two sentences of a literary work of no merit, by the time I reach page 199 I could go back to the beginning and delete the bit about the blank page. Don't be afraid to start!

Writing is a great way to live in another world. You can inhabit that world with monsters, heroes, pretty girls, scientists, handsome men, extraordinary places, wonderful events, totally unreal adventures and the only person you need to please is YOU.

You know what I want you to write first though, don't you? Forgotten already? I want you to write a letter to your, as yet, unborn great great grandchildren, and tell them about your father or mother. Your family for whom it is already too late to start writing. This is just a starting point. No-one will judge it, and it doesn't matter how badly written it might be, it will be wonderful to read in a hundred years' time. Best of luck, get writing.

Colin Bennett

Thanks Colin for a fascinating glimpse into your world.

Author David Barber has written more books than most people read in a lifetime and has been translated into numerous languages. He believes that many books are rushed into print far too quickly and without sufficient care to make them as polished as they should be. Here are his thoughts:

The Write Stuff
By David Barber

Anyone can write a book, but that's not the problem. The problem is that the old system of agents, ghost writers, editors and professional publishers by and large weeded out bad authors, keeping the standards of published work high and the writing profession something to be proud of. Britain particularly had a worldwide reputation for its commitment to excellence in all aspects of book publishing.

Where non-fiction professional publishers were concerned, they felt an intellectual responsibility for doing what they could to ensure that the content of their books was accurate by having drafts checked by experts in their field for accuracy. There was of course some self-publishing, but the cost of this put it outside the reach of the vast majority of people and it never became a significant part of the market. However, the few people who did self-publish were by and large either professional writers (such as Charles Dickens and many famous poets) or recognised academics, and fortunately for the profession they subscribed to and supported the high standards of both writing and publishing.

The advent of digital publishing and eBooks has changed all that. While many see these as a step forward in allowing literally anyone to write a book and publish it, the reality is that they feel no responsibility towards maintaining the proud traditions of either the writing or the publishing profession. If you will write and pay for it, they will print and bind it, or stick it up on the Internet, no matter how badly written or intellectually unsound.

In fact, digital publishers have no right to call themselves publishers. Middlemen with printers and book binders, yes, but not publishers accepting a responsibility for the quality of writing or the veracity of content.

Not all books that come out of digital printing or appear on the Internet are bad. But very, very few would not benefit from - and sometimes be completely transformed by - the ministrations of a conventional publisher. So this book is incredibly important because it plays a vital role and gives a public service in doing at least something to preserve the standards of book publishing.

If your work was being handled by a conventional publisher, all the immense amount of work involved in getting your drafts into a polished state suitable for publication would be done by the publisher. As digital publishers do not do this, what actually happens is that the vast body of work they handle is still in fact only in draft form when it appears in print. That would be considered completely unacceptable by a 'proper' publishing house.

So if you want to use a digital publisher and you have enough self-respect and pride to want to see your work reach the same high standard a conventional publisher would achieve, you must undertake to do the job yourself.

The vital importance of the editor

Why am I covering the need for an editor before going on to helping you to write your book? Because if you are not prepared to have your work properly edited, all the techniques in the world will not help you produce quality work. If you were that brilliant a writer, you would not be looking at self-publication anyway, because some mainstream publisher would have already snapped you up.

And you would still need an editor!

It is a myth that exists only among amateur writers that they "do not need an editor" or "an editor is not necessary." To some, the mere suggestion of an editor is taken as a slur on their writing ability. The only people who could put this situation right are digital and eBook publishers but, regrettably, this they fail to do, and this is the sole reason why the standard of writing in self-published work is so far below that in properly published books.

In fact, as any professional writer knows, the worst person to do the editing is the writer themselves. That is why, although the people who write for them are professionals, every newspaper, periodical and magazine has an editor.

For this reason, even the best known and most famous authors would not be seen dead without their editor. They consider them vital. In the trade, the editor is seen as important as the writer. Indeed, some authors, having found an editor they can trust, form a lifelong bond with them.

Even ghost writers, who in one sense are the most professional of writers, would think it inconceivable not to have their work edited.

So if you want your work to be knocked into the best possible shape then you too must get an editor. Or you can remain second rate, or worse. Your choice.

There are, it is true, some brilliant writers whose work needs very little editing, but even they value the improvements their editors make; at this level, even small editing changes can transform good into great, great into brilliant, and brilliant into genius. The fame of other writers actually owes more to their editors than to themselves!

Editors are in fact the unsung heroes of the writing and publishing world, and it is a tragedy that convention has not demanded that their names appear on the copyright pages in the way that film makers make a point of acknowledging all the craftsmen who make a film a reality. Maybe it is due to the ego of writers who would prefer to let the public think that their work is all their own.

If editors are as important as this in the traditional publishing world, then you should make them as important in your self-publishing world too. You should see them as integral to your own writing efforts.

In fact, with the right editor, you do not need to know any writing techniques at all because they will get your manuscript into shape for you. In other words, a good editor is far more important than any writing technique or ability you have.

Although the less an editor has to do, the lower their fee will be. Got the message? Then you now have at least a hope of producing a truly first class book, one that a mainstream publisher would be proud of.

Editors

A final word about editors. Theirs is a skilled science, and people who appear to be qualified are not. Aunt Flossie, knowledgeable though she is about the classics, is not. Nor is John, who belongs to a writer's (or reader's) circle.

Nor is Mary, who got a degree in English at Oxford. And I've seen too many books written by English teachers or lecturers who think that this automatically qualifies them to create expert work without the intervention of an editor - indeed, when it comes to book writing, they are no better than anyone else. A little knowledge (or, in their case, a lot of knowledge) is a dangerous thing!

The role of the ghost writer

Where ghost writers fit in is that the vast majority of books that are started, I suspect at least 99%, are never completed. If you have something you want to say but find that you too, for whatever reason, are unable to complete your book, then a ghost writer is your solution.

Using a ghost writer and then putting your name to the work is not cheating - far from it, it puts you in excellent company. Virtually all books 'written' by well-known personalities are in fact the work of ghost writers. Beyond that, you would be amazed at how many well-known authors in fact have their work written by ghost writers. So a writer claiming the work of a ghost writer as their own is a perfectly honourable and acceptable part of the publishing world, and infinitely preferable to the shoddy work they would have produced themselves.

There is, of course, a cost factor here but, if you cannot complete your book yourself and it matters to you to get your message in print, then a ghost writer is probably your only option.

David Barber

Many authors, (with some notable exceptions) are the worst people to proof their own copy. This is because their eyes see what was in their mind when they wrote it, not necessarily what is on the page in front of them. Zara Thatcher is a member of the Society for Editors and Proofreaders, and a member of the Filament Editorial team. Here are her thoughts.

Through the eyes of a Proofreader
By Zara Thatcher

If you have already written your book, then your next step has already arrived - getting it checked by a proofreader. When you are as close to a book as an author is, it is very easy to miss an error that is otherwise obvious to someone else. Here are ten reasons why you need a proofreader.

REASON 1   Spelling and grammar

This may seem like an obvious aspect to check but errors can still creep in. Spelling and grammar checkers are a useful tool but don't rely on them too much - they will not pick up everything. For example, if the wrong word is typed but it is still a correctly spelt word, the spell checker will not pick it up. A good example of this is 'there' and 'their'. Some spell checkers also use American spellings, which can be a problem if your publisher's house style is to use UK spellings. The publisher's house style sheet, which the proofreader usually receives along with the work, also states whether words should end in '-ise' or '-ize', when dealing with words such as 'realise'.

Do you know in which situations you should use 'a' or 'an'? A proofreader can check this too, as well as seeing which words should be hyphenated.

Homophones cause problems for many writers. Homophones are two words which sound alike but have different meanings and spellings, such as accept/except and affect/effect.

If the spellings of words are not checked carefully, these can slip in along with words where an extra letter may appear but can go easily unnoticed, such as 'acccountancy' and 'spellIng'.

REASON 2   Author's closeness to text

Authors have a closeness and familiarity with their work but this blinds them from seeing the flaws. But proofreaders are detached from the text so they have the ability to spot mistakes and inconsistencies. When we read, our brain interprets what it expects or wants to read, not what is there so fresh eyes are needed, such as a proofreader's, who is trained not to do this. Have a look at this:

I cdnuolt blveiee taht I cluod aulaclty uesdnatnrd waht I was rdanieg. The phaonmneal pweor of the hmuan mnid! Aoccdrnig to a rscheearch at Cmabrigde Uinervtisy, it deosn't mttaer in waht oredr the ltteers in a wrod are, the olny iprmoatnt tihng is taht the frist and lsat ltteer be in the rghit pclae. The rset can be a taotl mses and you can sitll raed it wouthit a porbelm. Tihs is bcuseae the huamn mnid deos not raed ervey lteter by istlef, but the wrod as a wlohe. Amzanig huh? And I awlyas thought slpeling was ipmorantt!

Another role a proofreader does is read from the same point of view as the reader so the proofreader will spot things that the author understands but the reader may not, such as unexplained terms or abbreviations.

REASON 3   Sentence and paragraph structure

This is actually something that a lot of people do not look at when checking their own work. There could be inconsistencies with how much space there is between paragraphs or if paragraphs are indented or not. When proofreading, a lot of people who are not trained at proofreading tend to read just the text, rather than look at the book as a whole. Headings and subheadings are easy to overlook as they tend to be written in capital letters, which makes errors harder to spot.

REASON 4   Missing words

Missing words can cause an embarrassing problem as spell checkers cannot pick them up. Missing out the "not" in "you should not connect this to a live socket" could have disastrous consequences.

REASON 5   Punctuation

A lot of people have difficult knowing where they should place commas, full stops and other type of punctuation. Can you imagine what will go through a reader's mind if you write "Let's eat Grandma", instead of "Let's eat, Grandma"?

Contractions, such as 'it's' and 'its', can cause problems with a lot of people getting them confused and using them in the wrong places. Contractions are also used to show possession and, again, you need to know where to use the apostrophe.

REASON 6   Inconsistencies

Some words have more than one spelling - for example, 'realise' and 'realize'. If you are writing both spellings within the books, you will then land yourself with inconsistencies. A proofreader is trained to spot these inconsistencies within the text by noting down words that may be spelt in different ways and how that particular author has been spelling it throughout their book.

REASON 7   Knock-on effects

By having a trained proofreader, you gain the reassurance that correcting errors will not cause new errors to appear. This is called the knock-on effect. This is where correcting an error could cause serious problems, not just for the rest of the chapter, but for the rest of that book thereafter. If the text is justified, correcting an error could cause bad word breaks in the rest of the text that follows, sometimes for the whole book. One example of this is 'manslaughter' becoming 'mans-laughter'! Here are a few other examples of bad word breaks:

therapist	becomes	the-rapist
reappear	becomes	reap-pear
legend	becomes	leg-end
readjust	becomes	read-just

Another knock-on effect that can occur is that it can cause errors in the paragraph lengths. If the last paragraph in the chapter ends at the bottom of the page, making a correction to an error could cause the last word or two of that page to move onto the next page on its own. This could then be repeated elsewhere in the book.

REASON 8   Photographs and illustrations

It is part of the proofreader's job to check that photographs and illustrations are in the best possible position. Sometimes, photographs and illustrations are not added until a later stage in the production of the book so can be easily missed out - a proofreader will alert the publisher if the image has not yet been added, in case it has been forgotten.

REASON 9   References and contents page

Due to copyright, it is vitally important that you have correctly listed your references to acknowledge the author of the original work. There are certain ways to set out these references, usually depending on which way your publisher prefers, but it is important that all of the details are listed correctly so that your readers can easily locate the original sources. Problems can occur when indexing references within the text, usually with the reference number being incorrect, and these errors can be hard to spot.

Contents pages are another common place for errors to appear with them not being checked thoroughly. Errors can be caused when anything is added to, or deleted from, the book, relating to the knock-on effect. This will then mean that the page numbers for the chapters that follow could be incorrect.

REASON 10   Font errors

You may think that once you have set the size of the type for the book, it will stay like this throughout the whole book. Not always. Computers have a mind of their own and any difference in type size that creeps into the book could be hard to spot. I have seen examples of work where authors have suddenly changed to writing in italics without realising it and didn't notice when they checked through the work themselves. Did you notice that I have just changed the size of this font halfway through this paragraph?

All these points are reasons why you need a proofreader. You will be secure in the knowledge that your book is accurate when it goes for printing. Having your work properly proofread shows your desire to have a perfect, error-free book, which will give readers hours of pleasure with no mistakes. It needs to be right for you and your readers. Critics reviewing your book will pick up on errors and this could potentially lead to a bad review, affecting the sales of your book.

Do not be in too much of a hurry to get your book to a publisher - an error could be costly, especially at a later stage. Make sure you have had enough time to get your book proofread and allow sufficient time for it to be returned and the errors corrected. The timeline will be determined by the date your publisher has set for when he needs the copy to reach him. Think wisely - get a good proofreader.

Zara Thatcher

Thanks Zara. Very helpful.

My Journey into Publishing
as an Author

By John S Rushton, The Life Alchemist

We all have something to say, we all
have stored knowledge and we all have
attributes that if not benefit ourselves
could well benefit others in similar situations. Life is like a large
chemistry set; what we do has an effect, just like putting ingredients
together to bake a cake. Everything is there, it just takes either us or
someone to put the right ingredients in place, turn on the oven, wait
a while and violà - we have a cake. It's not rocket science, in fact
baking has been a staple part of our very existence, but as we are
all different we have varying aptitudes as to what to do, how to do
things and perceptions and knowledge of why we do things, some
people are better at certain things than others.

Over many years I have written articles for magazines the world
over, broadcast via radio and television to audiences that I didn't
know existed, made CDs, etc., and from doing all this, I got positive
feedback directly and sometimes from the most extraordinary
places and contacts. I was by default accumulating a library of topics
that evolved from when I first started many years ago up until this
present time. These topics whilst in the same genre - emotions -
also evolved and the increased pressures in life today meant that
what I was talking about or writing about hit home in a more
pertinent way than it had ever done so before. Our emotions govern
the very existence of whom we are and our mental health is just so
important for if that starts to falter then our lives go to pot very
quickly and that's when our own world comes tumbling down.

I had in mind for some time to publish my collective works in a book, or books, but like many other things in life, it just stayed a notion in my mind whilst I continued to write for my global clients, adding even more potential but not realising any of it at all. This then changed, and like many a good thing I was recommended to contact Chris Day of Filament Publishing as to proceeding in the publishing direction, and a subsequent single call changed what was to what is, and the 'what is' is still an ongoing situation. From the first phone call, Chris took the time to identify what I do, the potential, the possibilities (and Chris is a vault of endless possibilities) and how to go about turning what I have into real books for sale and put the theory into practice. A subsequent meeting cemented the relationship between budding author and established publisher, and exchanges of information were made via email at a rate on knots.

Like anyone entering into 'unknown waters', it's all quite daunting, even though at the same time quite exciting too, but the reality of doing something that's ordinarily out of the norm makes at times the tasks at hand overwhelming and at other times a little off-putting. However, the Filament motto, like that of Mr. Muscle, is "we love the jobs you hate" which makes Filament, and in particular Chris, the star of the show in that he guides you through the whole process very smoothly and there is nothing en-route that can't be changed, altered, edited, revised, re-copied, re-formulated, or re - anything else. What we have as budding authors in our minds changes once we embark on putting our written scripts into book form. What we once thought is now different; we see that it needs to be tweaked here, moved there and so on. It's probably different for everyone, but from talking to other successful authors, it seems to be pretty much the same.

Self-publishing allows one to take things at a pace which is both conducive to one's own workload and time available so it can go as quickly or at a pace that's suitable and doesn't rush you into doing things that you may then regret. No matter what thoughts came to mind and what emails I sent to Chris, I always had a full explanation in simple terms that I could understand; even if on the surface my questions were basic, to me if I didn't know it was a potential block to proceeding forward. It's this attention to detail and understanding that gives the smooth flow forward, it takes the stress and strain out of "now what?" and smoothes the lines and eliminates those hurdles that one seems to endlessly come across when in unchartered waters; often such hurdles turn out to be relatively small or even insignificant, but if one doesn't know how to proceed they loom large.

Chris's knowledge of the publishing world and associated media is outstanding, and depending upon the subject content of your book, has many ancillary ways of getting your material published in various formats to maximise your potential and allow you to realise the financial rewards that can be had, as today we are quite spoilt in the way we look at and receive information from our chosen sources. There's nothing that can't be done with your book material and much of it is down to one's own preference as well and employing the technicalities that make one's written word or CDs accessible to the public via the many platforms available.

My first book was a journey for me; it was exciting and daunting. One then looks at what one has written and even challenges the content even though in hindsight it still has the quality that it originally had. Endlessly reading one's own material often makes one complacent and it takes the edge off what the content really means, although to others who have not had this previous accessibility it's all new and uplifting and interesting to them. In all,

Chris identified eight books worth of material from my 'back catalogue' of products, plus a wealth of ideas on how best to present each book via the myriad of formats. So now I've joined the ranks of accomplished authors, embarking on subsequent books, and at the same time I'm still writing more material for even more potential books.

However, it matters not whether one has one book or a hundred books, it's the fact that why let your knowledge live on a hard drive in your PC or a CD when it can be shared with those who are out there and will appreciate your subject content. The book market today is as wide as it ever has been and one has the chance to allow the public to choose what they read as opposed to being denied by those publishing 'gatekeepers' who judge on behalf of readers and often get it sadly so wrong in the process.

For those who are thinking or pondering or wondering or ever have a notion of being a writer / author and have thoughts such as "I'll get around to it sometime", stop right there, pick up the phone and discuss what you have in mind. It won't cost you a penny and it could just release what has been bottled up inside for an age. Chris will, I'm sure, even over the phone tap into what you have and unleash possibly for the first time an empathy with what you write about and the way forward; a way forward not, I may say, fraught with endless deadlines and emails from dozens of people demanding this and that, but a concise and tight and doable road which is only but good in concept and lives at your own pace. When writing one must be 'at one' with what is going on, otherwise everything will fragment, and then it becomes a chore and then it fragments. This will not happen with Filament and Chris will be your best friend giving you the impetus to make your desires in publishing come true. It's an empowering journey; it's a journey that also increases one's thoughts as to writing even more as it heightens the thought process although quite often one embattles with 'Spellcheck' as it says you can't 'write this' or 'that', but as an author you can write what you like in the way you like and the style that you like, that's the whole beauty about it. It's not regimented anymore, it's all free-flow and it's a part of you, it's what makes you tick and that's what writing is all about.

Out there, there are people who are awaiting your book, people who will enjoy the way you write. It will give them that feeling that "there are others like me" who enjoy what I enjoy. It's sharing on a higher level, a professional level, your chosen topic and the way it's presented to the world. It's not selfish, your book is a product just like a CD, a picture, a design, a restaurant meal; people are willing to pay for something that means something to them. People are even pleased that 'out there' they have found a gem of a product that has plucked their heart strings and it's nothing to do with marketing or hype, the content on its own merits resonates and has meaning; it's a standalone piece of work. Of course, the marketing and hype that puts your book in public view is essential to a large extent otherwise everyone may just pass it all by with the thousands of other books that are available, but nevertheless just having published your book is a feat worthy of praise and even self satisfaction, and a genuine one at that.

There are few companies, people and products that actually do what they say on the box, but Filament and owner Chris Day does just what it says. Chris has the ability to be a catalyst within our own lives regarding publishing in that he allows what we have to all come together and work.

The chemistry of our thoughts, written words, stored archives, ideas, ideals, aspirations, desires and feelings in this world he takes and adds that bit of 'magic' - the chemical that allows all to work harmoniously together and produces a product at the other end.

Living a life of wishing and hoping doesn't have to exist, you are just one phone call away from perhaps being the next best thing to Harry Potter?

John Rushton

Laying out your book on the page

For many authors, the way the text sits on the page and is presented is as important as the words themselves. The symmetry of the text, the way the headings and sub-headings are presented, the margins and paragraph breaks have to be done in a very specific way. And that's fine.

However, there is no point in wasting time with layout whilst you are still crafting the words themselves. Work on your raw text in whatever word processing programme you are most comfortable with. Many people use Microsoft Word, others use Word Perfect and a select band have crossed to the dark side and will prepare them on a Mac. Work on getting the words right first before even thinking about layout. It is highly likely that, whatever programme you created the original words in will not be the same programme that the book layout will be created in. Very often in transferring the text from one to the other, the finer points of the layout and formatting will be lost anyway, so don't waste too much time on page design until you are in a desktop publishing programme that is capable of producing files in a format that will be compliant with your printer's needs.

Having said that, you would never send a book to a printer in a file format that has not been 'locked' in place. Say for example, you have produced your book files in Word and had chosen a really fancy typeface. If you send that file off as it is, there might be the possibility that your chosen font might not be on the machine it was opened on, and a default typeface might be used instead. This could dramatically alter the number of characters on a line and throw the page layout completely. What you would get back might bear little resemblance to your original file.

Most printers will be happy to receive your book file as an Adobe Acrobat PDF document. PDF stands for Portable Document Format. Many desktop publishing packages have a facility to create PDFs. If not, you will need to purchase a PDF creator package to do this.

A PDF creator is seen by your desktop publishing package as a printer. You would print your document to PDF. However, it is important to get the setting correct before creating the file. More on this in a moment.

There are many creative ways of laying out a book in an interesting way. Before you start, it is worth spending an hour in a bookshop and looking for examples of publishers who have done this particularly well. There are many good design ideas to inspire you.

Spend a little time experimenting with typefaces or fonts, but resist the temptation to be too quirky. Make your book as easy on the eye as possible. If necessary, print out a few pages of your book in different font to see which you and others find easiest to read.

You will need to decide also on the formula for main headings and sub headings so that they are consistent throughout the book.

Choose also your preferred line spacing before you start so that this too is consistent. Personally I prefer a line spacing of 1.25, but it is your choice of what feels right for your particular title.

Another choice is to have forced text justification, where the text automatically adjusts to ensure that the right hand side of a paragraph is a perfectly straight line, or to go for a freer approach. Again, the choice is yours.

The 'trim size' of your book is the dimensions that the book will be 'trimmed to' by the printer. It is usually expressed in millimetres.

Book sizes

Most books are produced to a size between A6 (148 x 105mm) and A4 (297 x 210mm). There are three price bands for print on demand printing.

Band One - up to 234 x 156mm
Band Two - up to 277 x 204mm
Band Three - up to 300 x 219mm

For books printed on a conventional press, pages are printed in multiples of 16. If the number of pages in a book is not divisible by 16, there will be additional blank pages added at the back to make up the number. This does not apply to books printed using Print on Demand.

Papers

There are three different types of papers which we stock in a range of weights expressed in 'grams per square metre' (gsm). Higher grammage papers result in less showthrough (the amount of ink visible on the reverse of the page you are reading), higher costs and a heavier book, which may affect the cost of carriage if you intend to post books to your customers. The standard weight for cartridge and woves is 80gsm.

Book woves - a bulky paper available in both white and cream shades with a rough surface used mainly for publications containing text only (novels, poetry books etc.) or for low extent titles to give additional bulk. Not very suitable for reproduction of photographs or fine line illustrations.

Cartridges - a paper with a smooth white surface suitable for text and line illustrations.

Coated cartridges - particularly suitable for halftone illustrations on litho presses.

It is possible to use a combination of papers in a book, usually a book wove or cartridge for the text and art paper for a plate section.

Desktop Publishing

There are many desktop publishing programmes available. My advice would be to select a programme that has all the functionality that you require and that are likely to be used and known by the majority of people. This makes it easier to share your file with, for example, a proofreader, and editor or a designer, for them all to work on at different times. If you are doing this, always use the date in the file name to make sure you are working on the most recent version.

Start by creating a Master Page. The layout and content of the master page will be copied onto all additional pages. Further changes made to this page in the future will affect all other pages.

You should create a portrait A4 page which will need to be centred on all sides in the middle of the page.

The pages of your book are going to be printed in monochrome (no colour) so don't add spot colour to your pages - it won't be seen. Of course, it is possible for the book to be printed with digital spot colour, but this does add significantly to the production costs, and subsequently to the price you would need to sell it for to cover that. You can use as many line drawing, halftones or grayscale images you like, anywhere throughout the book.

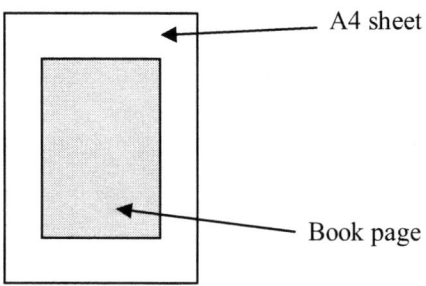

Using the 'guides' which can be created in your desktop publishing programme, create a box in the centre of the page to represent the trim size of your book.

Next, create a second set of guides which represent the margins between the edge of the page and your text. You would expect these to be around 15 to 20mm in from the edge.

Within this space, position a text box into which you will be pasting your content.

You will be linking the text boxes on this and subsequent pages together to allow the text to flow through the book, or at least through a chapter. This means that when you add additional line spaces at the beginning, it will have a knock-on effect across all the linked pages. This can be helpful when laying out the book for the fist time. It also means that when you go back to make changes or additions, you always need to start at the beginning and work through it, page by page.

Below the main text page, and above the guideline for the bottom of the trimmed page, put a small text box to hold the page number.

Be aware that every odd numbered page is a right hand page and every even numbered page is a left hand page.

Always start a chapter on a right hand page, even if the facing left hand page in blank.

Now, this is your book and you have total freedom in the way you lay it out, but there are some conventions you might want to bear in mind.

As you open the front cover of the book, the first thing you see will be a right hand page. This is page one of your document. You might choose this to be a blank page. Alternatively, many publishers will use this for reviews or testimonials. Certainly, when you are selling the book off the shelf, if the first thing that people read is other readers or even personalities saying how good the book is and what they learned from it, that can only help the decision to buy. So page one, and the page that backs onto it, page two, could be used for this. I have seen three or four pages of reviews in some cases.

Next, on a right hand (odd numbered page) will be your main title page. This should contain your book title, if possible in the same font that it appeared on the front cover.

You can also add any sub-heading that appeared under the title, and the author's name. It is customary to also have a small publisher's logo at the foot of the title page.

Backing on to your title page would be the imprint page. This would contain:

- The publisher's logo, company name, address, phone number and website.
- The book title
- The author's name
- ISBN number
- © The authors name and the year of publication.

Expert Tip - to use a © symbol, make sure your 'Num Lock' key is selected, then hold down the ALT key and type the numbers 0169 from the keypad. The © symbol will magically appear. Each font has numerous additional symbols, and letters with accents used by other languages. All can be accessed in the same way when you know their numeric address. There are shareware character map programmes available to help you identify the correct code for each letter or symbol, which can be found by typing in 'Character Map' in your search engine.

Also include on your imprint page:

- (The author's name) asserts the moral right to be identified as the author of this work in accordance with the Copyrights, Designs and Patents Act of 1988
- The name of the printer
- A copyright warning - there are many version of this, but a simple one will suffice such as:

All rights reserved. Copying by any means is prohibited without the prior written permission of the publishers.

Dedication Page

This is not an essential, but if you want to have one, it would go next on a right hand (odd numbered) page.

Table of Contents Page

This should always start of a right hand page, even if the facing page is blank. If it needs to continue onto a second page, this can be the reverse side of this page. If you have a table of illustrations or diagrams, this could be a continuation of the Table of Contents.

Acknowledgements

This page should come next, again on a right hand page.

Foreword

Do be careful to spell this correctly! It is not Forward!

Then eventually, once you have exhausted all of this preamble, you can start your first chapter - on a right hand page.

Now you are off and running.

Back Ups

Many desktop publishing programmes have the option of making automatic back ups of your document. Do check that you have enabled this feature. Also check that you know where these back ups are being placed. They are too valuable to mislay! Even when I have enabled this feature, I still manually back up at regular intervals. I know to my cost what it is like to lose a full day of writing with a computer crash. Don't let it happen to you! Keep your computer in good order. Keep your hard drive regularly defragmented and virus protected. Don't say you weren't warned!

When saving your documents, always use the date in the file name so you can track the version. This also means that if you did delete a passage and then think better of it a few days later, you can go back to the version before you consigned it to the electronic waste bin.

Creating Print Ready Files

Once your book is completed and has been proofread, you will need to output it in a format that is acceptable to your printer. Most printers are happy with a high resolution, black and white, PDF file to print from.

- Application files e.g. DOC and WPD are not acceptable to most printers.
- The best PDF is made from PostScript. Embed all fonts and deselect 'image down sampling' to ensure high resolution images are produced.
- Output resolution to be set to 600dpi. Electric halftones are fine.

NB. See www.adobe.com for creating files and also file information on downloading a good Adobe PostScript Printer Driver.

Creating your own PDFs

If you are uploading your own PDF, follow these guidelines:

- Fully embed all fonts used in the document. Take care that all fonts are only embedded once. Subsetted fonts over multiple pages can cause problems when your PDF is rasterised for print. Your document may be printed with symbols instead of fonts, garbled text or missing text.
- Set compatibility mode to PDF 1.3 (PDF 1.3 does not support transparencies and will flatten them when creating the PDF).
- Leave the PDF's colour space in its original profile. Do not convert CMYK to RGB or vice versa.
- Solid blacks will print solid at 100% with no other colours added. If you do add colours to improve the richness of the black, TAC (total area coverage) should never exceed 270%.
- Avoid very light colour builds of less than 20%. Below 20% tint variation is very difficult to control on a consistent basis.
- Turn off Overprint and Simulate Overprint
- The PDF file size should not exceed 700MB
- If your image dpi is greater than 300, downsample to 300dpi.
- Flatten your images.
- Flatten all transparencies.
- Do not use any security/password protection. The printer will not be able to print the PDF.
- Image compression should be set to ZIP if you want lossless (no artefacts/distortion-free) images. To reduce file size, use JPEG -> High. Do not use CCITT or LZW compression. LZW compression creates multi-strip images, which may show white lines when printed.
- If you are printing a colour book that has black & white images in it, the black & white images should have the colour space set to grayscale.
- The gamma of a grayscale image should be between 2.2 and 2.4.

Checklist

When your files are ready, use this checklist to ensure that nothing has been forgotten.

- Disk label with name, contents and contact details
- Original copies and files retained by you
- Hard copy output from the PostScript or PDF file provided
- List of files and positions in the eventual product provided
- Blank pages identified and included in your files
- All fonts have been embedded
- There is no mix of True Type and Adobe fonts
- EPS files incorporated use the same print driver as the final PostScript or PDF
- Customized fonts, if used, must be made known
- Illustrations and halftones have been included at full resolution
- Page size of the files is consistent throughout the book
- All pages are saved as single pages
- All pages have been saved to file, including blanks
- Bleed requirements have been considered when making page sizes
- Written details of any special instructions have been included
- All defaults for PDF work have been changed to limit compression and down sampling
- Tick marks, registration marks or crop marks have been included where appropriate
- All pages are in the correct order for the printing of the book
- Printer's imprint has been included
- When the PDF has been supplied, all fonts embedding has been set to maximum.

Cover Design

To successfully create your own cover design and print files, you will need to be fluent in a image manipulation programme such as Adobe Photoshop or similar. The same principles apply to whatever programme you choose to use.

Firstly, you will need to create a single file which contain the following items:

- The back cover
- The spine of the book
- The front cover

So to start, you will need to know the dimensions of each in order to create a blank document of the correct size.

The trim size you should know already. However, you will need to add a 3mm 'bleed' to the top, bottom and outer edge.

There is a formula for working out the spine width which is determined by the number of pages, and the type of paper used.

Standard ARL80 gsm paperstock - number of pages x 0.054mm
Bookwove - number of pages x 0.07
70 gsm - number of pages x 0.047
60 gsm - number of pages x 0.04

Example:

Say your trim size was 234mm x 156mm, and there were 100 pages printed on Standard ARL80gsm. You would need to create a document of:

Width - 3mm + 156mm + spine of 5.4mm + 156mm + 3mm = 323.4 wide

Height - 3mm + 234mm + 3mm = 240mm

It would then be wise to add guides to enable you to see clearly the position and width of the spine and where the cover artwork needs to bleed off the page.

It is the convention on the back cover to include an clear area which should include:

- Barcode
- Book Title
- Author's name
- ISBN number
- Publisher's logo

There are free barcode generators available online, which can be found using a search engine.

Remember, when converting your cover file to PDF:

- 300 dpi
- CMYK, not RGB
- No crop marks
- Not colour separated
- High quality setting
- Use A3 or SRA3 paper size

Cover Checklist

- Cover files in PDF form are usually preferred
- Make sure that you scan all images at 300dpi and save images as CYMK tiff or low compression JPEG files.
- Convert all colours to CYMK.
- Convert all EPS files to CYMK.
- QuarkXPress files for covers are accepted ONLY if all components such as images, fonts and logos are included in each title.
- JPEG is also an option but take care when saving to only compress at a maximum of 10.

Frequently Asked Questions

What is an ISBN?

An ISBN is an International Standard Book Number. Up until the end of 2006, it was a 10 digit number, but from 1 January 2007 all ISBN numbers are now 13 digits long.

What is the purpose of an ISBN?

An ISBN is a product number, used by publishers, booksellers and libraries for ordering, listing and stock control purposes. It enables them to identify a particular publisher and allows the publisher to identify a specific edition of a specific title in a specific format within their output.

What is the format of an ISBN?

Under the new system which started on 1 January 2007, the 13 digits are always divided into five parts, separated by spaces or hyphens. The four parts following the prefix element can be of varying length and are as shown on the opposite page.

- Prefix Element: For the foreseeable future, this will be either 978 or 979.
- Registration Group Element: Identifies a national, geographic or language grouping of Publishers. It tells you where in the world the publisher is based (not the language of the book).
- Registrant (Publisher) Element: Identifies a specific publisher or imprint.
- Publication Element: Identifies a specific edition of a specific title in a specific format.
- Check Digit: This is always and only the final digit which mathematically validates the rest of the number. It is calculated using a Modulus 10 system with alternate weights of 1 and 3.

Following the change on 1 January 2007 to using 13 digits, existing 10 digit numbers must be converted by prefixing them with '978' and the check digit must be recalculated using a Modulus 10 system with alternate weights of 1 and 3.

Do I have to have an ISBN?

There is no legal requirement in the UK or Republic of Ireland for an ISBN and it conveys no form of legal or copyright protection. It is a product identification number.

What can I gain from an ISBN?

If you wish to sell your publication through major bookselling chains, or Internet booksellers, they will require you to have an ISBN to assist their internal processing and ordering systems.

The ISBN also provides access to Bibliographic Databases such as BookData Online, which are organised using ISBNs as references. These databases are used by booksellers and libraries to provide information for customers. The ISBN therefore provides access to additional marketing tools which could help sales of your product.

ISBNs are normally made available in blocks of ten, not singly.

To purchase a block of numbers, you must contact the UK ISBN Agency (Tel: 0870 777 8712). Prices currently start from £75.00 including VAT. Further information about ISBN numbers is available on their website: www.isbn.nielsenbook.co.uk

What Binding styles are there?

Perfect Bound - Books printed by Print on Demand are done using a process known as Perfect Bound where a book consists of various sections with a cover made from heavier paper, glued together at the spine with a strong flexible glue. The sections are rough-cut in the back to make them absorb the hot glue. The other three sides are then face trimmed. This is usually with 90gsm offset for the text and 250gsm cover stock with a gloss laminated finish.

Limp Binding - Also called softback or paperback binding.

Cased Binding - Also called hardback or cloth binding. There are two main case binding styles: i) with a printed paper cover pasted down to the boards (also known as PPC binding) or ii) with cases made from imitation or real cloth and embossed. A jacket is optional.

Loose-leaf Binding - This is common for reference work where text may need to be easily updated. Pages are drilled for insertion into a ring-binder.

Wiro Binding - This is useful for reference books that are designed to lay flat (e.g. cookery books and workshop reference manuals).

Wire Stitching - Also called saddle stitching. This is used for magazines or low extent titles where the text bulk is insufficient to limp bind.

Next in this chapter, we look at the importance of good quality photography for your book and I have invited professional photographer Frazer Ashford to share his thoughts.

During the late 1970s and the early 1980s, Frazer gained a reputation for his imaginative rock and theatre photography. His subjects included such legends as Charlie Chaplin, Gene Pitney, The New Seekers, Rod Stewart, David Bowie, Elton John and Dr Hook with many pictures being seen in newspapers, magazines and books as well as being featured in one-man exhibitions around the UK and America.

Frazer Ashford has been awarded both an Associateship of the British Institute of Professional Photography and the Royal Photographic Society.

Never Judge a Book by its Cover - Wrong!
By Frazer Ashford

You should never judge a book by its cover - so we are all told over and over again. However in the real world nothing can be further from the truth.

Just think for a moment - if we never took notice of the covers, how come so much time is spent on producing record, CD and DVD covers? And how many times does the cover on a video game seem so much better than the game itself?

It is, I believe, especially relevant, ironically, to books themselves. How many times have we gone into a book store and picked up the books with the most appealing covers? If we are looking for a specific book, then we might be more focussed, but if we are just browsing and looking for either a gift or a present for ourselves, I believe that the cover has a major role in our book buying decisions.

Now, whilst buying a book or a CD might not be a life altering decision, just think about book cover appeal in our business life. Whether we are starting or running our own business, this 'Never Judge a Book by its Cover' idea must be considered when it comes to getting our message across, and gaining and holding customers.

I am not a complete cynic though as I do believe in the well-used saying "You only get one chance to make a first impression!" and in a way this actually backs up my thoughts about covers.

When you are trying to attract readers to your work, you have to accept that the competition is immense, whether your publication is designed to be found in a book store or on the Internet.

The whole trick is of course to make your publication as visually attractive as possible and it is usually entirely up to the cover. I don't actually know the statistics relating to how long book purchasers spend looking along the shelf but I bet that it is not that long - you must make your cover stand out!

So, what do we put on the cover? There is of course no simple answer and each book is different. Even within a narrow category such as cooking, you might find a 'back-to-basics' book features a great shot of the sun setting over an allotment. Another might show the finished vegetables in a great succulent close-up whilst another might feature a close-up of the celebrity chef involved.

A photograph is a great way to attract readers, but how do we go about it? I believe that the whole, and only, secret is to engage a creative professional photographer and discuss your ideas with him.

Once you have a few ideas sketched out, discuss it with friends, your publishing consultant and anyone that you think would have something useful to say, and as we all read books, it really does mean anyone!

You could even produce several sketches and ask friends to choose which is best.

Once you have your cover plan, work through the shoot with the photographer and turn your ideas into reality.

And how do we pick the right photographer? These six steps should help:

1)   Choose the right man or woman for the job

So, it is time to get some ideas on paper and get the pictures taken and a photographer is a photographer, right? Wrong! Creative photography is a very specialised job and when you consider that you may well be at the start of your career, success or failure may just depend upon getting the right type of photographs.

Look through some book stores, magazine articles and websites, and make sure that your preferred photographer is experienced in the type of image that you are thinking about. Many photographers are listed but they are not all good - far from it. One way to check is to ask for recommendations from others in the publishing business. Look at pictures on the book covers on your own bookshelves to see who took them and, probably the best way is to look through some shelves at the local library. I am not saying that you should copy other images, but you will get an idea of what is out there.

Certain photographers' names will keep leaping out at you. They are the ones to call. They may not be cheap, but do not scrimp on your cover pictures; they are your sales and marketing team all rolled into one.

2) Beware - most photographers are trained to take the wrong type of picture!

Photographers are trained to take the wrong sort of pictures! Well, from your point of view this certainly is a true statement. Most 'social/local' photographers take shots of people - happy people. They cover weddings, family groups, makeovers and portraits and with one thing in mind - to make the subject happy. Nothing wrong with that; after all they are in business to make money.

The more prints that the subjects buy, the more money they make. In fact many photographers don't charge for taking portraits and makeovers, they actually rely on the print sales.

And in order to sell prints they have to make their subjects look and feel good! Creative cover shots are not taken to make you feel good - they are taken to sell your publication to a complete stranger who is not drawn to your publication by a 'nice picture', they want an eye-catching picture with a bit of a WOW factor - it can even be shocking. This is totally the opposite of what your local regular photographer is aiming to do.

You need one good image, not sheets of contacts showing multiple poses! You should certainly get a good selection to choose from but the differences should be subtle - not vastly different! I cannot emphasise strongly enough that you are looking for that one shot - the shot that sells your publication.

So, whatever you do, do not go to a portrait photographer or use a mate. Take the advice in the previous tip and make sure that you use an experienced creative/advertising photographer.

3)   Keep it simple

Building on what has been said already, do keep things simple with your ideas. If the buying public do not understand your image they will move along the shelf or click on another item. A clear basic idea, well photographed, is all that is required. Excessive effects and a 'clever' image may well impress a portrait photographer or your friends but not the people that you need to sell to.

If your cover picture requires models, you must look at using professionals. It really does show. If you use an agency, then you will find yourself paying some stiff bills but it's crazy to spend your entire budget on the picture and no money on the subject!

However, a professional model may not cost as much as you might fear. Firstly ask around; you may find one that is a personal contact and might be willing to help you out - if not, there are several websites which specialise in bringing photographers and models together for mutual benefit.

One these sites - www.net-portfolio.co.uk - puts models who are looking to increase the diversity of their portfolios with photographers who need models. There are normally three different 'payment options' available.

Firstly, the models will need to be paid. However, the fees may well be considerably lower than using an agency.

Secondly, the models may offer to work for free providing they can use the final shot in their portfolio. This is a good option as it will not harm your publication and may well give you a bit of publicity.

The third and final option is that the model will ask for a CD of the images to use as she thinks fit to advertise her modelling. As you are only looking for one shot, it should not cause you a problem to let her have, and use, the other shots from the session.

However, you should discuss it with your photographer as he may have ideas of his own.

4)   Don't try to fool the buyer

Your cover image picture should portray the contents of your book! Nothing more, nothing less.

Most of all, it must be realistic. If you try to present an image that is nothing to do with your book, it will do you harm. You may make some initial sales but repeat business will not happen and valuable word of mouth may well work against you.

We have all had emails which persuade us to open them only to find that they are advertising some totally different product. Just be aware that the cover should attract people who are interested in the subject of your book and this is what you must give them.

5)   And only choose one picture

As explained earlier, portrait photographers want you to choose loads of poses - the more you choose, the more money they make. From a cover point of view, I hope that by now you will be getting the idea that your shot should not only be attractive to potential readers, but also be truly representative of the contents of your publication.

Whilst you may have several contact sheets or files to choose from, they should be reasonably similar. One should jump out at you and that is the one to choose. You could at this stage however, produce a few mock-ups to show others to gauge their reaction.

Your photographer should be able to assist you at this stage although with the help of today's computers, it need not be a difficult task to do.

Once you have decided on your image, and the relevant artwork is added, your photographer should be able to produce the final artwork in the required format.

6)   And finally

It can be tempting to cut corners, but potential readers are busy people and if your cover stands out, it may make them take a second look and hopefully take that final stage and purchase your book. Whilst you cannot make this decision for them, your cover image may well make all the difference.

Talk to a professional photographer in the first instance and then take it from there. They should not charge for a consultation if you are genuine. You may well need to employ a graphic designer to help out but I feel that the photographer should be your first point of call as you never know exactly what services he can additionally offer.

And finally? Whilst a great cover picture, based on the advice above, cannot guarantee your success as an author, it may well get your publication noticed and after that, as they say, you are on your own. Good luck.

Frazer Ashford
www.frazerashford.com

Part Three - Share what you know

There is One Way that you can ensure that you do complete your book - and it never fails!

It will always be far easier not to write a book than it will to write one. Statistics prove that the roads are littered with people who have started to write and then found that doing anything else was far more preferable. However, there is one sure way of making certain that you stick it out to the end - and that is to go public.

If you are a niche author, one of your greatest assets is going to be your social and business networks. These will be your first customers, and your greatest fans. They will share the fact that they know a published author and be great referrers of new customers to you. Once you go public to them and they know that you are writing a book, there is no going back.

Your network and your list will become, in time, your most valuable possession. The time to start building that list is now - well in advance of your publication date. After all, they will be your first customers.

They say that the world is divided into two groups; those that use social media and those that don't. Which ever group you are currently in, there is no doubt that this is an area you will need to become proficient in if you are to succeed in raising your profile. Certainly there is no cheaper way of doing so. There are a number of different social networks and more are coming on stream. Each of them appeal to different groups. For example, www.ecademy.com has been established as a business network for over a decade and attracts users worldwide. Then there is LinkedIn, Plaxo, Facebook and Twitter to get your head around. Each is a world of its own. You'll probably be surprised when you join to find a good number of people there that already know you or know of you, so you will not be starting out cold. Using social media has its own etiquette and rules, so get familiar with the culture before jumping in with both feet and causing too big a splash.

David White, the founder of Weboptimiser Ltd, is an industry expert in this area and advises businesses on the strategic use of social media to drive traffic to their websites. Take a look at www.weboptimiser.com Here, he shares his advice on how you can build your list.

Is Social Media relevant to business?

By David White

This article provides a quick lesson in fine tuning your email writing skills with a twist. That twist is Social Media.

I am often asked - "what is the one thing I should know about internet marketing?" It is this: email marketing.

The reason is sending messages, whether it is via Facebook, LinkedIn, Twitter or via an email client, is still the most effective thing that you can master online.

Email marketing is the cornerstone of Social Media, as it has been for the life of the entire online industry. It was the first killer app - and it is still the greatest.

At the end of the day, everyone uses the system you are about to read. It is therefore the most essential system to learn and really is the only system you need to know.

The success of email marketing stems from the fact that it is a form of direct response marketing. Direct response marketing is in essence where you write to an individual with a message and you ask them to take action.

Like Social Media, through email you have a conversation with the person you are writing to and through email, it is very personal.

There are many, many sales examples of using words to sell. Famously there is Joe Sugarman who sold millions of BluBlocker Sunglasses using off the page advertising using very few photographs, filling most of the space with a headline, subheads and copy. His system still works today in email. Before the Internet there were three primary formats for Direct Response: advertising in print, advertising on television (infomercials) and direct mail.

Email's nearest cousin is direct mail. Unlike direct mail, email is free to send - no stamp, no envelope, no printing, so we have three outstanding benefits straight off. The biggest difference between email and direct mail is that you do not use email to sell directly.

There are a few reasons not to sell directly. The first is that you want your emails to be read. If your emails are always sales emails then you will create a reputation that you are always peddling something and so your emails will simply not get opened and your value will diminish.

If I had a dollar for every time I have heard "the 'fortune' is in the list", I would be a multi-millionaire. They are right, the 'fortune' is in the list. I will show you how to get that fortune in this article so there is no need to blow it.

You do not need to worry about the size of the list. I have known of many occasions when colleagues have had small lists and made big money.

One reason for success with a small list is that if your list is extremely targeted and your communication is always about that target niche, then your value to the reader is much higher.

Email marketing applies to every business; b2b, b2c, large or small - any and all!

Fact is, as you will see, it is not hard to possess the knowledge of how to grow and profit from opt-in lists.

Keep on reading - you can pretty much write your own ticket when you know how to put this stuff into practice. Let me tell you how it works.

I am going to show you how simple it is in one word. You should know it was Jimmy D Brown who gave this one word to me first: PROFIT.

Top Tip: You should use acronyms in your business. You will see how to use the PROFIT acronym here.

With just one simple easy word - the best word of all - PROFIT - we will focus the essential ingredients that will improve your sales prospects for life.

I suggest you take a pen and paper and write what follows down. Taking notes whilst reading is a key tool to learning from what you read. Also, in this case, you will end up with a checklist in your own writing that summarises this article that you will be able to use forever.

Down the left hand of your page, write out the six letters P R O F I T. Simple stuff.

I am going to explain the PROFIT acronym in my own unique way. What follows is my take on it that no one else uses based on real experience and sales achieved. Here goes:

Next to P - Promote your list

Next to R - Reward each member

Next to O - You have to offer something

Next to F - Focus attention

Next to I - Initiate a response

Next to T - Thwart the filters

Now, I am going to explain what I mean. So, on with the show...

P - Promote your list. You need to get people to your site so they can join your email list and give you permission to begin mailing to them.

You need to send mail to them super fast, as they will soon forget who you are and if you leave it too long they will forget and think you are spamming them. You don't want that to happen....

Seriously, the best thing you can do is to get people to join your list - the 'fortune' is in the list. Your first priority in all your marketing online and offline activity is first and foremost to build your list. The purpose of everything - your website, pay per click, banner advertising, even your email advertising - is indeed to get people to join your list.

When you see or hear the word 'traffic', think 'list', otherwise your traffic will pass you by and you will have a ton of visitors and no email addresses because no one had any idea about what they were doing - let's make a nice website, let's get visitors through PPC or SEO, why? To get visitors to the site? No, to get sign ups to your opt-in list.

Don't buy a website design unless it allows people to add themselves to your list. It is the most common element missed out - simply absent from most websites.

Most websites either go straight to shopping cart or, just as bad, 'contact us'. As a minimum you should have a phone number on your page - this is the most common form of contact that site visitors will make. Then you need to ask permission and add them to your list.

Don't sign off your emails without a link for people to sign up to something... they will - this is not rocket science.

On www.weboptimiser.com there were at one time three ways of signing up on every page. My colleagues thought I had gone too far, but we have a ton of people signing up every day - how else do you think we got to a multi-million turnover?

Don't use PPC or advertising to promote an offer - promote your content as bait to build your list.

Do this and you stand a serious chance of super improving your short, medium and long term sales for your business.

Collect email addresses of interested parties and your business will grow.

Just in case the penny has still not dropped (my fault) imagine this. If you send good information to your list often and nicely with respect, so much so that people write back with thanks or leave comments on your blog, then you have a list that loves you.

Do you think it is easier to make sales to a list of people that love you? Do you think that if you regularly stay in contact with them that when they are ready to buy they might buy from you? Do you think if anyone they know is planning to buy that they might recommend you?

Let's move on, back to your notes. Next to R - 'reward each member'. Reward each person that signs up with the information you offer.

You could offer a webinar, a newsletter, although they don't work so well nowadays, or a report - I prefer those, they still work very well.

You need a great title. Most titles are really positive - '4 keys to successful Internet marketing' or '4 essential techniques to avoid the costly mistakes and pitfalls of internet marketing' - which do you think is more effective? Well you will never know until you test them...

You need some trust. Twitter works well here, as it is expected that you post a picture of yourself, and what is more trustworthy? A picture of you or your business's logo. I have tested it and the picture of you wins over.

Twitter is Social Media, Social Media is all about having a conversation with people, therefore it is personal media.

Take a separate piece of paper, write down at the top left of the page the word Beginning. In the middle of the page to the left write Middle. Toward the bottom of the page, to the left write End. You now have a simple content framework - bonus!

Under each of those three headings, write down a handful of bulleted points. Four to six items, write everything down. We are not editing yet. The biggest problem when writing is to edit as you go. It is not until you can see the whole thing laid out in front of you that you should even begin editing.

Here is another bonus: take a separate piece of paper for each section and you may well have started to form a chapter by now. But this time, on the separate piece of paper, write out the bullet points, put the best first and the second best last. That way you start on a high and you end on one - making it worth reading to the end. Also if you show the bulleted list, at a glance it will read better.

I learnt the bullet point technique when writing for website users and indeed search engines would you believe.

O - make an offer they can't refuse. The key is to make an offer that really is a no brainer to your visitor. You want them to opt-in to your sales process. At that point, you have to make it ever so worth their while!

Now I do not propose that you say "buy this" or "buy that" as in B U Y. If you do, then it is going to end up as Bye Bye, as in B Y E - you don't want that...

In my case, I either offer something direct or I introduce others, as I tend to meet lots of people who have got interesting ideas. I tend to introduce those and they in turn either sell something or offer a free information orientated call or something like that.

I have also asked my list for feedback, their most burning question and even asked for top tips and testimonials, as well as recommendations and experience. So it is not all about selling.

Your list is not just about customers. Our list has a life of its own and I am always being introduced to people as a result. It affects my network of influence and I have discovered that my network are forgiving; they will tell me when I am not hitting the mark and tell me when they are really excited.

So far we have covered P R O, PRO, Promote, Reward and Offer, next up is F for Focus - Focus attention so that your readers actually open the email.

This is a major feat that you need to think about carefully.

I have just in the last week sent out an email that had great content, but had a lower open rate because I did not craft the subject, which is in effect the headline as well as I might...

This is a tough one, yet this is one of the most important areas.

If people do not open your email, you are doomed doomed - er that was for lovers of *Dad's Army*, just giving away my age there...!

So for instance, mention a price or that there is an offer and your open rate drops sometimes, but usually, especially if people think you are sell, sell, selling...

A top tip would be to dig out all the emails that you have opened and look at the subject lines of those. That is what my inbox is for!

People like how to, top tips and warnings... it needs to be as short as possible. One of my most opened emails was 'weird, isn't it?' So you can definitely add intrigue to the list.

Paul Evans over at Simple Six suggests that you open a gmail account and sign up to all your competitor email lists and see what they DO, not just what they SAY.

You can search for sites on Google using your target keywords and just as easily sign into sites who offer a newsletter simply to see what is current, what is being said. Hotmail and Yahoo both have lists that you can sign into.

I like watching out for lists that have bit.ly links. The reason is you can see how many people react to their headlines using the bit.ly analytics...

That is a top tip taken straight out of the social media top drawer.

OK, what we have done so far, we have covered P R O F, PROF, Promote, Reward, Offer and now Focus.

So next is I - I for initiate a response.

We are going to talk about useful but incomplete, just like this article. I hope you are finding this useful. There is some genuine content here and this content is absolutely the system you will use for email marketing inevitably. The acronymic way of laying this out is beautiful and I hope you are loving it as much as I am talking about it.

Now as I am writing this, we are in February, I am influenced by the big day coming shortly: Valentine's Day.

So this is useful but incomplete, in other words throughout I have explained the key points and alluded to there being more information available - I can and do go to much much more depth in my articles, in which there are many.

Your email should do the same. Genuinely provide some of your best and most useful ideas. I think the PROFIT system is one of the best and most useful ideas that I learnt from Jimmy D Brown, I have also been reminded about it by Paul Evans at Simple Six who has a great book on the subject.

Paul says in his book, "If you learn nothing else from this lesson, learn this: the real secret to getting staggering results from your email marketing is to make a difference in the lives of your list members by giving them something they can use..."

Put your best ideas forward first. Don't worry about being copied; there's way more under the hood and they are the type of things that you can only know by being an active practitioner...

So finally, T - Thwart the filters. This is the last hurdle, it is absolutely key... You have built a list, you have delivered on your promise, crafted an offer they can't refuse by focussing on their needs and provided a way for them to initiate a response...

All we have to do now is to make sure that we get it to them. If they never saw your email, there would be no point in any of this...

Who is to blame, the system, your competitors, you or the subscriber? Well the answer is all of them, every party is guilty. Subscribers will forget that they ever subscribed and they will delete you and or hit the unsubscribe button. The systems don't like certain keywords like FREE, your competitors may mail too often and too weakly.

You may be guilty of sending an email that is too salesy so that the email fails either the electronic filter or the human one...

You can't do much about most of these things. But you can play the game when you need to.

You can confirm you are real when you get challenged and for that reason I always give a real email address, so that I can confirm I am a human to those that employ spam guards.

You can ask subscribers to approve - or white label you. All they have to do is to get an email from you and save you in the list of known email addresses - this helps a ton.

Paul says you should send the odd email as a PDF attachment.

So there you are. I hope you found this information interesting and useful.

Remember this system uses the acronym PROFIT because we cover all the angles, with P - Promote your list. R - Reward each member. O - You have to offer something. F - Focus attention. I - Initiate a response. T - Thwart the filters. They are the sales steps necessary in any sale scenario, so it's essential for every business and I have just walked through the complete reality of using email marketing in your business and indeed any business.

You know it is so simple, but most people, even I at times, forget how essential email marketing is, how it sits at the very core of what we do and yet sometimes it is the last thing we do with the least amount of care - and in the process ruining our chances of developing our business to grow to greater heights and that is why I have shared this with you; it really, honestly, truly must not be missed, this is the essential ingredient - and it is all within your power, within your grasp and it is free to deploy, as often as you want.

Like the long distance runner, you only get to win the race when you have practiced and practiced to hone those skills.

I have made it so you do not have to wait for the most perfect weather, I have made it so that you can follow this checklist, so that you can re-orientate your business, so that email marketing takes centre stage and as a result you will beat your competition to your clients and grow your business in a nice way, with verve and enthusiasm.

David White

Marketing your book – and then some!
By Ron G Holland
author of The Eureka! Enigma - 7 Keys to Realizing Your Dreams.

Having been a published author for 32 years I feel I know a little about marketing and promoting books; especially those that are niche market, non-fiction.

I have been published by major publishers like Harper Collins and also self-published, and have also used many PR agencies from Max Clifford to others who specialise solely in book promotion. Now I want to make a sweeping statement that I think will hold you in good stead no matter where you fall in that spectrum. You must take responsibility for creating your own major stories, image, marketing and credibility. A tall order I know, but I am going to show you how to do it, in great detail!

Create your own image and re-invent yourself as you go

I love Madonna and she knows more about re-inventing herself than anyone I know. You must do the same. Come up with a handle that puts you immediately at the top of your own niche. When I had my motorcycle breakers yard over 40 years ago, I was King of the Breakers; now as a consultant, I am Top Biz Guru and as a seminar leader, I am Britain's Leading Motivational Speaker.

You have to do this bit yourself!

So what's your niche and your own self-appointed title? Are you King of Marketing, World Renowned Expert of Sales, The Tastiest Chef in the World? No one wants to buy a book from someone who isn't an expert in the field and at the top of their game so you have to create that impression and buzz. Don't expect someone else to do this for you - even if you pay them! Have some fun with family, friends and colleagues, and see what exciting, attention-grabbing title you can bestow on yourself. Are you the next Dog Whisperer, or the next Chef of Chefs? Perhaps you are an Internet Cash Machine or Money Wizard or The Entrepreneur's Entrepreneur which I have been called many times and called myself that even more times... get the picture? You need to work on this and have fun with it and be outrageous, audacious and self-appoint yourself with a great marketing title that rings in people's ears. You can always change it as you go along and as you get into different niches.

Articles work - when you know what to look for!

It does take a little work and effort to write an article but the paydays are big. I've been at it for over 30 years now and if it didn't work, I wouldn't do it! Most people miss the point about articles but I'll share some gems with you. Each article may only produce one sale, but if that person happens to own a large company or network you could begin to fly. Not only that, most books are sold via word of mouth. Sell one copy and s/he then tells two friends and so on, and suddenly you've got the tiger by the tail. When I send a book out in the mail, I always enclose two advertising flyers for the book in the package, hoping they get passed on, and invariably they do. Articles can be cut out, copied and sent to prospective clients. I have a portfolio going back many years full of gems, front covers and stories that I copy from time to time and send out. The accumulation effect is awesome and that preponderance of 'evidence' more often than not helps create big sales with big players. Many times, prospective customers need to see a name or a title over and over again before they buy. I know this from personal experience. I had to see Joe Karbo's advert for *The Lazy Man's Way to Riches* five times before I bought it; and I'm glad I did because it turned my life around - as books often do!

Keep feeding articles out there!

You have to take the initiative on this one and keep trawling magazines, newspapers and of course the Internet in your own niche and sending out articles, making phone calls to see what is needed and generally making yourself very busy. Make sure that each article relates in some way, shape or form to the specific book that you are pushing at the moment and also ensure that the article elevates you to the top of the tree in credibility and information that you are divulging. See that each article you get published is a part in the 'jigsaw puzzle of success' and when you have enough out there the world will know who you are, and even if not beat a path to your door, will certainly buy your book in sufficient numbers to make it all worthwhile.

The biggest gem of all - bar none!

Always remember that your book is not your business. It is a calling card, a credibility builder and a massive door opener. When the door is open, hopefully you'll do what all the other gurus do in their respective fields; and that is sell consultancy, workshops, seminars, coaching, mentoring, training, manuals, audios, DVDs and other products and services that all revolve around your books. That is where the big money is - never forget it and remember where you heard it first!

Ron G Holland
www.eureka-enigma.com and www.wealth.co.uk

Public Relations

There is no use in having the best book in the world if nobody knows it is out there. Of all the many ways of raising awareness, PR is one of the fastest and most effective. The trouble is that everybody believes that they are a PR expert. It is only when you come face to face with someone who actually is that you realise that good PR is both an art and a science, and there is far more to it than is generally believed.

To help authors to better understand what they can do themselves, and what is best outsourced to an expert, I asked my friend and colleague Ray Hodges, a specialist consumer and business-to-business Public Relations consultant, for some guidelines and creative suggestions on how authors can mount an effective PR campaign for a new title... and this is her response:

Mounting a PR Campaign
By Ray Hodges

Those who practise it consider that PR is an
art, and it takes time to learn the best ways
of setting about getting what is called 'free
editorial' coverage - whether it is in the
press, on the radio and TV, or online. Every time I mount a PR
campaign for a client I start from scratch - going through a number
of processes to make sure I present the offering (whether it is a
product or a service) in the best possible, and most interesting, light
to journalists and broadcasters. In this business, there is no such
thing as a 'standard' PR programme.

Let me take you through the various steps involved:

Identify your markets

You wrote your book. As well as knowing your subject, you also know
to whom the book will appeal. List all the different categories and
types of prospects to ensure that your PR programme will be correctly
targeting the people most likely to end up as purchasers of your
book. Then think outside the box - are there other, linked markets
where people just *could* be interested, or people who are opinion-
formers, who could start 'word-of-mouth' going about it? It's worth
considering targeting them, too.

Establish your messages

Sit back and look at the book carefully. What are your most important
messages? What will people, as individuals, get out of buying the
book? Will it help them improve themselves? Will it help their career?
Or help *their* business? Write those messages down, and if possible

identify some of them as being unique to your book - people won't buy it if they don't think it could provide 'added value' to their life, or their livelihood.

An 'official launch date'

If you are serious about making your book a commercial success, you need to agree a 'launch' date with your publisher. As you are self-publishing, it is best to set that date at least a couple of months after you get your first copies of the book to ensure that it is in reasonable distribution, and also that your website is set up to take orders.

If you are lucky, and a major High Street or online retailer takes the title, they may ask for an initial 'exclusive' period (where they put the book on sale before any of the other retailers get hold of it). If this is the case, they will probably be prepared to help you promote the title, including organising advertising and PR through their own in-house resources.

They will also sometimes set up a book tour or signings within their outlets if they think your messages and the appeal of the book are strong enough to attract the attention of both the regional media and their customers.

Timings

When planning your PR campaign, an understanding of the lead-times on the various categories of media is imperative. You'll want to obtain the most possible exposure at exactly the right time, so it's important to work out (and work to) the lead-times for the various types of media in which you're looking for coverage.

These are the usual timings to work to:

Monthly glossy and business magazines	3 to 4 months
Trade and specialist journals	1 to 2 months
Weekly and fortnightly publications	1 to 2 months
Weekly and Sunday newspapers/supplements	6 weeks
Television and radio	4 to 6 weeks
National daily and regional newspapers	1 to 3 weeks
Part-works, features, specialist supplements etc.	Up to 6 months

These days, online coverage is of major importance - many of the biggest, most influential websites and national news portals have literally millions of visitors a month. Surfers looking for specific information or help are also just the right sort of people for you to catch, to tell them all about your book. But be a bit careful; website editorial can be instant... you don't want the coverage appearing too early!

Media material

The main means you will use when contacting the media is a press release. This consists of a maximum of three or four pages, written in the third person, which summarises the content of the book. The press release needs to be descriptive rather than boasting, laid-back rather than too commercial. And the better it is written, the more likely it is to catch the interest and admiration of editors and writers, researchers, presenters etc. who are extremely busy people.

If possible, identify a really interesting or topical angle - and flag it up in your headline. You'll need to sum up the whole book in the first paragraph - then you can go into more detail in the following pages. If you have received endorsements for the book from third parties, include them.

Writing a good, attention-grabbing and informative press release is not easy. If you're not sure how to do it, buy a book on PR... it will have examples of different types of release, and provide a structure from which you can build your own creation.

Make sure you include your website address within the press release. Contact details for yourself (offering your availability for personal or telephone interviews, email Q&As etc.) should be positioned at the bottom of the last page.

Illustrations and photography

An image of the front cover of your book must appear on the first page of the press release, and if it contains illustrations or cartoons, a few of these can be placed in suitable positions within the text. If you have a good picture of yourself (it's worth having some portrait shots taken professionally) it should be placed alongside a short *About the Author* section, which should not be more than ten lines long.

Media contacts

By far the most difficult facet of 'do-it-yourself' PR is making approaches to suitable media. PR professionals (recognised PR consultants or full-blown PR agencies) have access to computerised contact lists of anything up to 25,000 different journalists and broadcasters, all categorised both by type of media and individual job title or specialisation. They also have their own personal (and favourite) contacts - often freelancers who are experts in a huge diversity of subjects - who they can draw on if they think a particular story will appeal to a particular person.

You will be starting more or less 'from scratch', so the best way to do this is to identify which are the magazines, programmes or websites you would most like to see covering your book. For magazines, buy a copy - and you'll see that the names of the most important writers are usually listed in the front section. For TV and radio programmes, you'll need to contact their station or production company individually to get the right names.

For consumer media, it's important not to address your communication just to The Editor or The Producer. That shows you haven't bothered to find out the right person to contact... and it's not impressive! For trade and technical magazines, you may be able to get away with just contacting The Editor (by title) - because some of these types of publications are really quite small, and the Editor will probably control most of the published content.

Media approaches

A good PR consultant or agency doesn't just send off hard copy press releases or bulk emails. The way approaches should be done is to personally contact at least 20 of the writers or broadcasters who you consider to be your prime contacts - usually by telephone first and then with a follow-up email. This should repeat the main thrust of your telephone conversation, and of course the press release will be attached, and sometimes it is also a good idea to attach a PDF of a couple of chapters from the book (which your publisher will be able to provide).

If the person then comes back to you for more information, or asks for a finished review copy of the book... it is likely that you have scored! Respond politely - but don't go overboard, and whatever you do... don't keep calling or emailing your contact to see what is happening. They absolutely hate that!

Press and online coverage

It is most likely that your book will attract the interest of journalists working in the press or on websites, for placement either in their 'What's New' or Book Review sections. However, it may be that 'serendipity' kicks in, and that your approach is timely, so that you suddenly find you are being asked to provide opinions or comment for a feature the writer has in the pipeline. Or you could be asked if you'd like to be included in an article on your particular subject, which is currently being prepared. In return for your input, it is usual for the name of the book to be included, and at the end of the item your contact details/website address (for online purchase) will almost certainly be listed.

If the subject matter or your book is of particular interest to a publication, you may be asked if it could be made into a 'highlights' or 'digest' feature - or even used as a part-work. Again, you will get a good name-prompt if any of these methods are applied... and for part-works you would be entitled to ask the Commissioning Editor with whom you are liaising with for a fee for allowing them to feature your intellectual property, if the copy used is over a certain number of words.

If you are truly an expert in a particular field, you could also approach your trade press or local newspapers offering to write a weekly, fortnightly or monthly column based on your own knowledge and experience, with or without a Q&A section. The latter could make you into a bit of a local celebrity, which will almost certainly enable you to get your book into many local outlets - and not just book shops. An inexpensive plastic dispenser positioned near the till of a number of neighbourhood shops will reap small, but regular sales. 'Every little helps'... as they say!

Broadcast coverage

The UK has a huge, proactive network of both independent and BBC radio stations, and many of the regional TV operators are also often on the lookout for interesting news about local personalities. It is quite likely that there are at least two independent radio stations as well as a BBC one in your immediate area... so they are a prime target for your approaches. Just phone in and ask the switchboard for the names of the researcher or producer of the programme which you feel would be best for you - drive time is always good, as programmes going out as people commute to and from work have the highest listenership of the day, and the highest proportion of business people within their audience. Many of these stations are quite small, so you may even be put through to the presenter (if he or she is not on-air) - and that's always a bonus.

TV is obviously much more difficult, and probably the only way you can expect to be featured would be if the content of your book has a topical resonance or is controversial. Or you could perhaps tie in with a current national or regional news story or constantly evolving topic, such as global warming, personal finance, learning, health or age issues, child welfare etc.

If it is about empowerment or personal development (and you have an attractive, characterful and charismatic appearance and personality yourself), you could get lucky with a major chat show or one of the regional or national women's interest programmes. And if you are a business writer, the BBC's lunchtime programme *Working Lunch* is a good place to be, if what you have to say is strong enough and interesting enough to attract their researcher's interest in the first place.

Products as prizes promotions

An extremely useful tool for expanding upon the coverage you are likely to obtain for your book is to organise giveaways or competitions, particularly with consumer publications, websites and local radio. Here, you will need to find the name of the person who is responsible for promotions within their team, and 'sell' him or her the idea - offering a number of your books as prizes.

The prize value (at retail) required will normally be around the rate card advertising equivalent for the space involved, which can be anything from an eighth of a page to a full page, depending on the format of the publication or website. For websites and radio stations, around five copies are usually sufficient. There are also many other promotional opportunities available, such as Subscription Offers, Letter Page prizes, or even providing books as incentives to enter the Completed Crossword or Sudoku competitions run in the nationals.

Capturing coverage

It is very unusual for a newspaper or magazine to send you a copy of 'your' piece in their publication, although if you ask them, most websites will send you a link for checking, before the item goes live. If you want to track what press coverage you are achieving, you will need to sign up with a cuttings service, which will invoice you for a monthly 'reading' charge, plus around £1 per cutting achieved. Their minimum contract is usually of three months' duration.

Also, radio and TV stations are much too busy to provide disks of 'your' piece, so you will need to organise to record these items yourself. If you achieve national coverage, but don't pick it up at the time, you can contact a national monitoring service within a month of appearance - and they will send you a DVD for you and the family to keep for posterity!

To sum up, Public Relations is not a black and white, 'effort equals certain success' scenario. A great deal of work can be put into the media approaches, but at the end of the day, it's a bit of a 'you take your horse to water, but you can't make it drink' situation. If your target journalists and broadcasters don't like your book... you won't achieve coverage.

Don't despair, though... if they DO like it, they'll enthuse about it themselves, in print, online or on-air. And suddenly many, many thousands of people will know all about it, in very positive circumstances - and a proportion of them will, without doubt, be prepared to buy the fruit of your labours! Good luck!

Ray Hodges

Ray Hodges has thirty years' experience in the PR field having run two successful and nationally recognised PR agencies. She now operates her own 'PR boutique' out of the HPS Group, one of the biggest marketing communications agencies in the south of England, specialising in consumer leisure and business-to-business PR. Past and present clients include 3M Photographic, the Automobile Association, the British Potato Council, Cadbury, Columbia TriStar, De Beers, Marks & Spencer, Nintendo, Procter & Gamble, Erno Rubik (inventor of the Rubik's Cube), the Seafish Authority, Tony Buzan (creator of the Mind Mapping technique, international lecturer and author of over 100 books), Vauxhall Motors and the Whitbread Beer Company.

Ray Hodges and her multi-talented and highly experienced team offer a 'budget' PR launch service (of three months' duration) to new authors, or can mastermind and operate an ongoing full-service publicity programme for those already established in their field. To find out more, you can contact Ray on 01628 894793 (direct line), or email her at r.hodges@hpsgroup.co.uk.

Radio Interviews

There are one hundred and sixty eight hours in every week - which is a lot of time to fill if you run a radio station. As an author, you are of interest to a radio station. You have something to say. You have a point of view. You have an insight into a topic of interest to their listeners.

Your task should be to indentify the radio station, the programme and the presenter that is likely to be the best match for you and what you have to say. So don't rush to send out hundreds of impersonal letters to every radio station you can find an address for. Take them one at a time. Find out the best person to speak to. Telephone them to seek their advice. Tell them about the book and be prepared to send out a press kit. Bearing in mind they are a radio station, if you have a recording of a previous interview, send them a CD so they can hear how you come across. It will help.

Practice first on some small local stations to build your confidence and to practice being interviewed. Make sure you get a recording of it and learn from it. You will get better with practice.

When you have the date and time of a radio interview, promote it to your email list. It gives you more credibility in their eyes. You can then put extracts from the interview on your website as a podcast.

You could offer product as prizes if they were to run a competition for their listeners. They are always looking for things to give away!

Don't forget, the more audio material you build up from interviews, the more you have to draw from for audio products to sell alongside the book.

One author who has a great skill in giving the media what they want - and getting great coverage in return - is the top business guru and international author Ron Holland. Here are his thoughts.

How massive book sales are really created!
By Ron G Holland

Find a strategy that works for you

I have been a published author of business and self-help books for over 32 years and want to share with you what I think really creates sales. For a start, I do know it's different for every author and every book, and you have to work out a strategy that works best for you. When *Debt Free with Financial Kung Fu* came out in 1977, I used full page adverts in many magazines, including *Exchange & Mart,* and sold the book off the page. I got the writing bug and moved to America in 1979 to become a full time writer and wrote *Talk & Grow Rich.* When the book first came out in 1981, it started selling slowly in the book stores. Acting on my own initiative I sped things up by getting the book into the hands of many Diamonds within the network marketing industry. To do this, I went to the main library in Boston and got literally hundreds of names and addresses, and sent out a sample book. As a result of that massive energy and effort, multiple orders flooded in.

One phone call turned my life around

I was surprised to get a phone call one day from a Diamond in Newark, New Jersey saying that all his group had now read the book and loved it and would I come and do a motivational talk for them?

I asked him to tell me a little more. Apparently they would pay me, fly me to New Jersey, put me up in a swish hotel and also help me sell as many books as possible. Of course, I found myself saying, "YES!" However, when I put the phone down, reality hit me. I had never talked in front of a group of sales people or distributors in my life. The most people I had ever talked to at one time was probably a dozen or so when I had my motorcycle shops back in London when we had regular jazz up sessions and mastermind group meetings with all my mechanics and salesmen. But this was different. I was now going to be speaking in front of hundreds of people, and I was the author of *Talk & Grow Rich* and a guest speaker!

I visualised the scenario over and over again and then I had a Eureka! My big idea was to set up my living room with 30 empty chairs and start practicing. I made notes, created motivational stories directly from *Talk & Grow Rich* and added many jokes and anecdotes. I then proceeded to tell the 30 empty chairs the whole one hour talk over and over again. As I practiced I kept honing up the pitch to such a degree I could actually 'see' imaginary people on the empty chairs, hooting and hollering with my humour and getting enthralled with my motivational talk. I carried out this crazy practising for about two weeks, right up until the time I was due to leave Boston and depart for Newark.

Suddenly, I really am a motivational speaker!

When I arrived at Newark, I was warmly received and put up in the best hotel. On the night in question, I was introduced as a celebrity and for the next hour I belted out my motivational story, every joke, every sales tip, every punch line... exactly as I had done for the 30 empty chairs, which was my full previous and entire experience of public speaking. When I was done, there was rapturous applause and the organiser pulled me to one side and said, "Well Done!

I didn't realise you were a professional public speaker - do you mind if I pass your details to other Diamonds and other networks who may want to use your public speaking services?" With that, I got on with signing books, shaking hands and exchanging business cards and have been at it even since.

I ask if I can speak at events!

These days I still find that speaking engagements offer the very best opportunity for any non-fiction author to start selling his or her books. These days I still get asked to be a guest speaker, but the truth is I also put myself about and actually ask to talk at events, and you can do the same. When you see an event advertised where you think you may be able to contribute a 15, 30 or 60 minute slot, pick up the phone and ask the organiser. Say that you're happy to come along and do a slot to add to the mix and all you need is a table at the back of the room where you can put your books and sell them. Yes, you'll get a few rejections, but on the other hand you'll get enough "Yes"'s to keep you very busy and sell a lot of books. I also have an ample supply of brochures and business cards, and also sell other products, audios, consultancy and workshops. You need to realise, the big money is often not made on the day, but with back-end sales. To develop this idea further, it's not a bad idea to develop a 'speaker sheet', which is usually an A4 sheet with a picture of your book, a headshot and bio of yourself, a little bit about the book and what you talk about. Use full colour and don't forget to include all your contact details. This can be sent out as an email or as a flier in the mail. If you send me an email to topbizguru@hotmail.com I'll be happy to send you my 'speaker sheet' so you can get a clearer idea.

A few more clues and tips

With a little research you'll find many potential events where you can speak at. Start with Google and look at companies, magazines and distributorships that pertain to the title of your own book. Most authors forget why they wrote the book in the first place and it'll do you a power of good to track back and think of your original ideas of who you thought may buy your book in the first instance. For example, does your book have a place within network marketing or direct sales companies or mail order firms? What about art and craft shops and indeed specialist book stores, museums and schools? The other thing you should do is set up a little mastermind group of a few people who may be able to help you find speaking engagements, sell books and create multiple marketing ideas. I've been doing this for a long time and couldn't get by without my group. It massively enhances your power and dramatically increases books sale - and that's what it's all about!

Ron G Holland

www.eureka-enigma.com and www.wealth.co.uk

Marketing the book

Of course, the Internet is the best place to search for anything. It is a shop window open 24 hours a day in the living rooms and offices of billions of people worldwide. The more specific and targeted your site, the more likely it is to be found by people sharing that same interest. Of course, you need professional help to ensure that your site is easy for search engines to

see, and that its contents are really targeted to your niche interest group, but these days none of that is expensive.

The object is to build a virtual community using your website and to use the site to interact with them and add value to their experience. You want to be seen as an expert in your field and the place for people to turn to when they need to know.

Don't be misled into believing that once you've built your site that the job is done, and you can sit back waiting for the money to roll in. If only! If your site doesn't change, it is a 'Cob Website', and will not attract repeat visitors.

Everything you have on the site should encourage interaction and repeat visits. Here are some suggestions:

- Testimonials and reviews
- Press cuttings
- Biographical information on the author
- A blog
- A discussion forum
- A facility to subscribe to an ezine - an electronic newsletter
- Articles - background on your book, where the inspiration came from, why you were moved to write it
- Links to other sites covering the same subject
- News items from the press on the subject
- Details on book signings or live events you are appearing at
- Photo gallery
- Your recommendations of books on the same subject by other authors

Most importantly, your site needs to have a stunning free offer on it that can only be had by the visitor entering their email address. The most important feature of your site is its ability to generate leads for your email marketing database. This facility needs to be on every page.

All of these elements will cause people to come back and visit the site regularly. Make sure you have enough additional things for them to buy, like the audio version of the book, a DVD of an interview with the author or tickets to a training event you might be holding.

Of course, you need an ecommerce facility so that you can turn your visitors into customers. This is the main place where you will sell your book. A simple shopping cart is all you need with a payment vehicle, like PayPal, to collect the money.

The Newsletter Trap

At one time or another, most authors will contemplate creating a monthly newsletter to send to their database. It usually seems like a good idea at the time. Not that they have anything startling they want to say, but instinctively they believe that it would be a 'good thing' to do.

So without any particular strategy and with no real objective in mind, other than to 'communicate' with customers, they make a start. The first thing they discover is that, despite the fact that they have successfully written a book, writing a newsletter takes far longer than they thought, and it wasn't easy to even fill a single page with interesting and relevant copy. But they persevered, completed it and emailed it out promising monthly editions long into the future.

Four weeks later, and it was a really busy week. More work than they could handle so, not surprisingly, the newsletter got pushed back a further week. But, it did get out. Not quite as big as the previous one, but who's counting.

The month after that, well they took a holiday, so instead of four weeks, or even five weeks like last time, on this occasion the monthly newsletter turned into a seven week newsletter. I'm not going to tell you about the next edition, because everyone was on holiday, and it just got forgotten. A not uncommon scenario!

But now, looking at this from a customer perspective, what message is being communicated? It is a fact that any individual or organisation is communicating at its loudest and most effective when it is saying nothing. Unfortunately when it does say nothing, the message received by customers is that it doesn't care about them. In a world of noise, when we are bombarded with messages from the moment we wake until the moment we go to sleep, when a business stops communicating, the relationship it had built up with its loyal customers, is in grave danger of being lost. Other businesses, who communicate better, will be in the forefront of a customer's mind, when they are ready to buy - not yours.

When you promise a newsletter, you have made a promise. You and your business will be measured by how well you keep your promises. When you fail to deliver on such a simple promise as a newsletter, what else will you not deliver on? Only choose to do a newsletter if you intend to deliver one - without fail, every time. If not, it can be more damaging than not doing it at all.

So if that's the dangers, how can you make it work? For an example of what works and what doesn't you don't need to look much further than your inbox. How many newsletters and ezines do you receive that get deleted before you even open them? So why don't you open them? One word - Relevance! No relevance equals no interest, followed by delete.

Most newsletters fall into the trap of looking inwards rather than outwards. They are full of the company talking about itself, how good it is and how clever its graphic are. But a few do get it right.

There is one I actually look forward to receiving. It is full of useful industry news that has been collected by this particular company, and intelligently presented into a series of short news items with links if I need to find out more.

Because the information is interesting and relevant, I read it. What is more, I feel positively towards the company who has taken the trouble to put it together. They are providing a useful service to their customers and are positioning themselves as industry experts at the same time. If I am looking for the type of services they provide, I am far more likely to give them the opportunity than not.

In a competitive marketplace, knowledge is a currency. Providing your customers with regular hints, tips, and topical and relevant industry news is a great way of maintaining profile in their eyes.

People tend to buy from those they know, like and trust; in other words, from a business they have a positive relationship with. Being a source of valuable information can give you a definite edge.

Every time you have contact with your customers, it needs to leave a positive mark in their mind. A regular newsletter, well crafted, and delivering on its promises, is just one way of achieving this.

Getting tangled in the web

To really own your niche, it is the Internet that needs your real focus. Many authors complain that, although they have a perfectly good website, which has the book prominently on sale, it doesn't generate the results they were hoping for. It generates traffic - but not sales. Why is that?

Very possibly because other people do exactly what you do yourself. They find out about a book from the author's website, but then search on Amazon to see if they can buy it cheaper. And very often they can because Amazon discounts everything to the bone. Good for the buyer, but no good for the author. So what should you do? Play them at their own game and discount it yourself? No! That can only be a downward spiral.

The more you play the discounting game, the cheaper you will sell the book, and the less money you will make. But there is a bigger danger. When you discount your own title, what you are in fact saying is that you don't believe your book has value. If you don't believe in it - why should anybody else?

Adding Value

I believe in price integrity. The price of the book is the price of the book. However, when selling it on your website, what you can do is to add additional value that they can't get anywhere else - including Amazon. Create an Added Value Bundle. This might contain a free CD of an interview with the author or a 50% discount off another product if they buy the book today. You could bundle in a Free Report with the book or a free download of a workbook or companion volume. The choice is yours as long as it creates clear blue water between you and Amazon.

But if they do buy the book elsewhere, and hopefully many people still will, what you do need to build in to it is a device to ensure that they visit your Landing Page website. The big value of the book is in the additional sales it can generate for you online. So always include in the book - even on the cover - an offer of a free download or a companion product from the website. Of course, once they get there, they need to give you their email address in return for the free download. Once you have that, you can include them in your email marketing or pre-programmed auto-responder sequence to enable you to develop that all important long term relationship with them.

Never forget, your email list is your most valuable asset. There is no point in having a website that people can visit and leave, and you have no idea who they are. It is a total waste of time. Far better to create a series of Lead Generating sites, each focused on a particular need or keyword covered in the book. The purpose of the site is to build your list and you do this by offering the visitor something valuable to them, which answers an important question, or provides them with some useful information, in return for their email address.

A Lead Generating site should have a domain name linked to the information you have on offer. For example, if your book was all about investment, your Lead Page site could be www.seven-top-investment-mistakes.com (don't bother visiting it, I just made it up!). It would offer a report about the seven biggest mistakes that investors commonly make. It would be a free report, and sent automatically to them by return, in return for their email address. This then goes into your database, and triggers a sequence of pre-written emails from you.

Using one of the many email marketing systems, like www.mailchimp.com www.aweber.com www.constantcontact.com or www.infusionsoft.com the recipient of your report then receives a series of personally addressed, relevant emails providing them with useful information. At the same time they start to build a relationship between you and them. As people tend to buy from people that they know, like and trust, this starts that process. It is also the time to let them know about your book, the other products that are relevant to them, the events you are speaking at, and the courses you provide. It is a step by step process.

However, most authors are impatient, and want to go straight for the sale, and don't see the value in building a relationship. You can either make a sale or create a customer for life. Both require different strategies, and both offer very different rewards. Do you know the value of a lifetime customer? Whatever it is in your world, it has to be vastly more than the value of a one-off sale.

Many people think that by simply having a 'Sign up for our free newsletter' facility on their website it will do the trick for them. They are the ones who have traffic to their site and who have no idea who they are. Everything you do on the web has to be focused on building your list. Well-serviced, it is that list that will generate the long term relationships with the people who value what you have to say - and will be first in the queue when your next book, product or course becomes available.

When is a book not a book?

It is very interesting to see the increased awareness about eBooks and digital editions. The demise of the physical book has long been talked about, but despite all technical attempts to kill it off, it remains as robust as ever. The first paperback book was pioneered by a German publisher in 1931 and, despite the launch of the Kindle and the Sony eReader, paperback books are still as popular as they ever were. What has changed however, is the marketplace, the ways books are bought, and the many new ways that we can all access information.

Whilst the industry as a whole has yet to come up with a common formula for the relationship between physical books and electronic editions, every publisher is more than well aware that everyone has their own preferences for the way they receive information. In today's busy world, many of us are deprived of the old fashioned pleasure of curling up on a comfortable chair in front of an open fire to enjoy a good book. Instead, we grab brief moments travelling on the underground, or commuting on the train. Other's preference is for the spoken word; after all, we all love to hear a good story. For them, a podcast is the answer, downloaded onto their iPod and enjoyed whilst cycling. Talking books are also popular in CD format for those who drive regularly.

Back in 1768, the first edition of Encyclopaedia Britannica was published in weekly parts. A novel way of publishing then. Now, with handheld devices becoming the window into their world for a huge number of people, there are already publishers who are providing their titles one little chunk at a time to be read on their small screens. There is truly nothing new under the sun!

The lesson is that, publishing a book in a single format, only as a paperback for example, is going to exclude a large number of people for whom that is not their preferred medium.

The more savvy publishers are now releasing their titles in multiple formats to suit every type of reader. You can now read a book in hardback, paperback, in all of the various eBook formats which require different file types for each, as talking books on audio CD, chapter by chapter as a podcast and a few more besides!

Some authors are taking a leaf from Encyclopaedia Britannica and are publishing their books online, on their own websites, chapter by chapter, as they are written. When the book is subsequently completed, then it is ready for the other media.

So whatever media you originally write for will be doing both yourself and your readers a great service by ensuring that your material can be accessed in all possible ways. Far from being an extra expense, it will open up additional sales opportunities you may otherwise have missed. It will also give you a competitive edge in the marketplace, because other authors with competitive titles may have yet to wake up to this opportunity.

The book is far from dead; in fact it is all these other media that will ensure that it is around for many decades to come.

Joint Ventures

Some of the most successful businesses started with little or no money for advertising and promotion, but grew quickly through setting up joint ventures with synergistic partners. If you were selling wood, for example, the perfect partner would be someone selling woodworking tools. So if your book was about getting out of debt, a perfect partner would be an author writing about setting up in business.

With any joint venture, it has to be a win-win situation for both parties. No money necessarily needs to change hands and it might all be done on a handshake and a promise. If you have a connection or relationship with a potential partner, that is a great way to open the door. Start with people you know or who know you.

You are looking for someone who has a mailing list who would be prepared to either include an endorsement of you, an article by you, promotion of your event or product, or to provide a link to your Landing Page site (not your website!). In return, you offer to do the same either now, or later when your list is bigger. When both products or services naturally go together and don't compete, it should be an attractive opportunity for both partners - and a positive benefit for their customers.

And finally....

Did you know that, in the United States alone, there are eight hundred new books being published every day? If you look at worldwide figures, you could probably double that. If you then add all of the eBooks and other electronic publications that emerge on the Internet, you begin to get the picture. I don't share this with you to depress you into thinking, "So what's the point of publishing another one?" but instead to focus you on what you need to do next.

If you have written something that you believe in;
that you have spent long hours crafting;
that you have shared with people whose advice you respect;
that you have made the best you can make it;
and you have written it to help people to gain insight into a subject and add value to their lives,
then you can congratulate yourself on a job well done.

Unfortunately though, it is only half the job.

Right at the start of the book, I invited you to have a clear idea as to your "Why?" - your purpose for writing the book in the first place. I suggested that if just writing the book and having a copy in your hand was all you wanted to achieve, then it would be a bit of a pointless exercise.

Always remember your "Why?" because that is what will help you really focus now on achieving it. Your book is going to open doors for you that you may not have been able to even get close to before. It will cause people to think differently of you - hopefully for the better!

It will move you closer to achieving the big goal that becoming a published author was a stepping stone towards. But only if you get the next stage of this journey right - and it is going to have the same ups and downs as you experienced writing the book in the first place. Having only just finished your first journey, you are about to embark on your second, and it will be just as challenging, but a lot more fun!

Books are meant to be read. They are meant to be shared. To be lost and then rediscovered years later. To be enjoyed. To be studied. To be full of notes and scribbles. To take you on a journey of discovery so you can become better, more informed, more capable of a performing a particular task, or just to help you to gain an insight into something new. Books are not meant to be written and then ignored. They get very upset.

As an author you not only have the responsibility to make your book the best it can be, but also to make sure it reaches the people who you were writing for. They need it, and your task now is to make sure they know about it.

Nobody owes any of us a living, so do not expect anyone else to have the same passion for your book as you do. Your book is a transference of your passion for your subject to the reader, so if you cared enough to write it, then you need to put that same passion into marketing it. It is your responsibility to make it happen.

I strongly believe that after decades where the balance of power was with the publishers, and authors often came off worse, the tide has turned. The comparatively recent phenomenon of search engines has changed everything. Instead of businesses needing to spend money to raise their profile and to attract the attention of a potential customer, the customer is now searching for them. All you need to do is to be visible to them, and that is far far cheaper.

For an author of a book that is aimed at a niche audience, this could not be better news. It is now cheap and easy to develop a worldwide following online by creating a website focused precisely on the one thing they are searching, for which your book provides the answer.

But outside of the web, you also need to do everything you can to use your book to raise your profile within the world that your potential reader inhabits. You need to be seen where they hang out. They need to realise that you are indeed an expert on your specialist subject. This is no time to be shy and retiring!

Earlier in the book you heard from Ron Holland, who is not only a great author, but he has also developed the art of marketing himself. Be inspired by what he has achieved, but realise that you too can do the same. You don't need to ask anyone's permission. Your greatest asset is your enthusiasm and it is what will motivate others to find out more about you, and hopefully buy your book!

Put yourself in the mindset of your potential reader and really get to know your niche marketplace. Look for every opportunity to contribute content to websites seen by your potential reader. The same applies to magazine and other publications. Put yourself about (as they say!) - it is what authors need to do.

Also never forget that words are the building blocks of all products. Not everyone reads books. Some will listen to them on a CD in the car, or as a podcast on their iPod. Make sure your words are available in every media to meet the needs of everyone you are trying to communicate with.

On the web, it is also important that your own family of websites, (yes, one is not enough!) are designed to resonate with the words and phrases that people are searching for. Don't be afraid to share information and use it strategically to build your list. It is this that will be invaluable in the future when you come to sell companion products, seminars, online courses and, of course, your next book!

Happy writing!

"To know,

and not to do,

is not to know"

So, what are <u>you</u> going to do now?

If you would like some practical

advice or support with your book project,

go to www.AskChrisDay.com

where you can download some free tools and

find information to help you with your project.

You will also find news of Chris's author's

workshops and training events

To be continued.....